HOW TO IMPLEMENT
CHANGE
— IN YOUR —
COMPANY

- so everyone is happy with the results!

JOHN SPENCER · ADRIAN PRUSS

PIATKUS

© 1993 John Spencer and Adrian Pruss

First published in 1993 by
Judy Piatkus (Publishers) Ltd of
5 Windmill Street, London W1P 1HF

**The moral right of the authors
has been asserted**

A catalogue record for this book is
available from the British Library
ISBN 0–7499–1258–8

Edited by Carol Franklin
Designed by Chris Warner

Set in 10 on 12½pt Concorde roman
by Phoenix Photosetting, Chatham
Printed and bound in Great Britain by
Biddles Ltd, Guildford and King's Lynn

CONTENTS

PART III   TOOLS FOR CHANGE

FOREWORD

We all face change every day – in transport timetables, in our workplace and in our families. Major change, thankfully, doesn't occur every day but even small changes can cause upset unless they are well handled. John Spencer and Adrian Pruss tell us in this book how to avoid such upsets. They explain how to anticipate when change is coming, how to prepare those involved in the change and how to help them through it. They also show how important it is to develop an atmosphere that *welcomes* change.

At BP we have been facing an enormous culture change process. We followed many of the principles set out by John and Adrian and our experiences reinforce many of the messages in this book.

From experience at BP, my most important advice in change management would be 'Never rest on your laurels.' Always monitor what the competition is doing, what your customers need and how society is changing. The Human Resources changes we made in BP were thought by the majority of line managers and HR staff to be revolutionary madness. There was little awareness that top companies across the world had been introducing similar programmes for the last decade as we slowly dropped down the league.

Such blindness to external changes makes it a very bold person who leads this change process. The more needed and far-reaching the change, the more internal opposition there will be. Evidence suggests that such leaders have to be expert at kicking-off the process, but other skills are needed to keep the change going forward. Witness Gorbachev, Lenin, Martin Luther King, Margaret Thatcher and Robert Horton. Courage to lead long-term change is often scantily rewarded.

How do we help people respond positively to change? The key needs, as the book identifies, are information and a feeling of being able to make a contribution.

I believe that change is not the same as uncertainty, and it is the latter that really worries our employees. The difference between the two is information. By explaining what an organisation is trying to do and how that will impact on teams and individuals, and by counselling employees through their fears and concerns, we can bring understanding to all parties. Sadly this is a skill which managers seem not to possess in abundance.

And perhaps employees can contribute something to decisions on what might usefully be done differently. The book's analogies between organisations and the military are interesting. Schizophrenia is rife among the workforce in the western world. At work, many companies consider employees unable to contribute to discussions on 'how things should be done around here'. Then, after work, these self-same people go into a self-managed team where they are responsible for taking decisions on cash flow, investment, work organisation, people management etc. These teams are, of course, families – and most of them are very successful.

As John and Adrian point out in *How to Implement Change in Your Company*, many organisations claim to be a 'family'. I feel that most companies that claim this have forgotten what a family is really like. Every family I know has at least one 'black sheep', one 'health problem', and a wide cross-section of ages and levels of intelligence. A happy family learns how to reconcile all these various differences and is always ready to 'forgive and forget'. When companies actually work out for themselves how to operate in a similar way, they will be able to realise the full potential of their total workforce.

You will find an excellent chapter on culture. One aspect of industrial culture in the western world troubles me. We seem to reward most steps forward in efficiency by reducing personnel. What incentive does that give an employee to make a positive suggestion to improve the working of an organisation? Or a line manager to propose how best to strip out a layer of hierarchy? Is there a way of changing this mindset? Perhaps the book's chapter on outsourcing points a way forward.

The book is full of good advice and practical ways forward. Based on my own experience at BP and at British Coal, I would like to reinforce their advice in three areas.

Firstly, never skimp on allocating resources to training and the time to talk through, and listen to, all the issues surrounding the change. Our maxim at BP is that we want all our employees to have the highest levels of skill – sufficient to walk into a job in any other company – but we want them all to be motivated to stay with us. How can a company be the best in the world if the employees are second-class in terms of skills?

Secondly, it is vital that all the supporting systems in an organisation – promotion policies, pay systems, budgetary mechanisms, delegation authorities etc. – reward those who are championing the change. For example, if more team work is needed then don't have all the reward systems tied to individual performance.

Thirdly, change is accepted more easily if the leaders are trusted. In families we put much emphasis on trust as a virtue to be valued. Such trust must be earned; once lost, how difficult it is to regain. John and Adrian tell us much about building trust that we would all do well to take to heart.

I recommend this book to all current and prospective line managers and HR professionals. We all have to cope with change every day at home or at work. The practical advice and guidance given by John and Adrian will help us to see things through without anyone noticing that anything has changed.

David McGill
Manager, HR Strategy Development
BP Chemicals

INTRODUCTION

Change is not an aberration, disturbing a normally stable world. Quite the reverse. There is *no* stability; change is *always* happening.

To the individual, change may not always be apparent, particularly when it is the sum of small changes experienced; it is none the less real. To a Roman soldier standing guard on Hadrian's Wall the fall of the Roman Empire (i.e. change) was probably inconceivable, but tiny and often unnoticed changes were nevertheless occurring that eventually did lead to the fall of Rome.

In times of great stability the pace of change is slower than it is during periods of turbulence. In unstable times, such as war, the pace of change has to be accelerated for the sake of survival; usually more resources are given to change projects during this time. For this reason all wars have created great progress; the Soviet and American space programmes were a direct result of rocket development by the Germans, who were searching for more powerful weapons during the Second World War. It is sometimes only with the perspective of hindsight that we know whether change has been beneficial or malign; the success of change in the business world is similarly measured after the event. The challenge to the individual in business is to design change that has the highest probability of a beneficial outcome.

If we look again at Rome under the stable conditions of the Pax Romana, change must have seemed slow, may even have been unobservable at the time, but history teaches us that great change was happening then, in literature, law and social development.

From our perspective at the end of the twentieth century, the years before the two world wars appear to have been very stable, with low inflation and low interest rates, and Britain retaining control over sources of raw materials throughout the British Empire. Since the Second World War, however, the pace of technological change in the world has accelerated. The observable, unstable environment has created a desire to put back some stability into the system through trade agreements, the establishment of trading blocs and the construction of economic and fiscal groupings such as the European Community.

The temptation of business managers has been to try to isolate the business from change; to create a stable environment in the organisation capable of resisting change pressures from outside. This has always been a hopeless and wrong-headed approach which only ever seemed to work when change was slow. In modern, fast-changing conditions its failure is all the more obvious.

The task of the modern manager, then, is not to resist change but to welcome it and to manage it. Indeed, once the constancy of change is recognised then effective management incorporates change into all of its planning; this is the fundamental principle of the management of change.

Towards the end of *Alice in Wonderland*, Alice is invited to play croquet. When she learns how to swing the croquet mallet – and just as she is about to strike – the mallet turns into a flamingo. When Alice learns how to swing the flamingo – and when she is about to hit the ball – the flamingo lifts its head. When she learns how to swing the flamingo – and take account of its lifting its head – then the ball turns into a hedgehog. This could serve as a model of modern industry and commerce facing corporate change; just as individuals are mastering new technology or working methods, so change occurs and they have to adapt and relearn. In this book we shall show that change is a learning experience for individuals; managing change is planning the learning and monitoring the outcomes.

At the present time change is something to which we have become so accustomed that we often give it no more than a passing thought; men on the moon, reusable spacecraft, computerised technology and medical breakthroughs are all things we take in our stride. A generation born into a world of such advances readily accepts *technological* change but they, unlike those before them, will also have to face tremendous demands for *attitudinal* change in their work environment. This is a challenge that is still quite radical, and possibly the last 'change-barrier' yet to be broken.

WHAT DO WE KNOW ABOUT CHANGE IN OUR ORGANISATIONS?

We know that change is often resisted and that people appear to prefer the status quo, but equally we have become aware that all is not as it appears. Actually people *like* change, it is the *method* of introducing change that they resist.

In this book we look at the effects of change on management and employees, as well as customers, suppliers and other stakeholders, and how we can overcome resistance to change. We evaluate how to identify the present culture of the organisation, and how to construct and deliver the new culture that will be necessary for the long-term growth and survival of a business. We demonstrate how change should be managed, drawing from our experience as change agents and, more recently, as change consultants in multinational companies and smaller organisations; we look at how effective change plans can be conceived, planned and implemented.

We know that planned change is usually introduced to find a way in which the organisation can function more effectively, utilising new information and resources. In order to introduce change easily, managers must take great care to develop the appropriate behaviour in their staff so that they can continue to be effective and innovative. We also know that in all too many instances change occurs after – rather than in advance of – the need for it. We know that change is a learning experience for individuals, so we consider how we can introduce and train for change in the employees' preferred learning styles; employees' past experiences and present beliefs have a strong influence on acceptance of the processes.

In our experience the most effective change is initiated from the top, but with consideration for the effect of change upon employees, who must therefore be part of the planning process. We have identified that change is more successful with highly motivated individuals, so part of the preplanning for change is to identify and remove the barriers that hinder acceptance of change.

We also look at how to monitor change and when to arrest certain changes – at least in the short term – in order to avoid overload and rejection.

In all change projects the attitude of the leader is critical, indeed more so than the change itself. History has many examples of leaders who have had strong – sometimes bizarre – beliefs, but who have been able to introduce real change by their ability to deal with people. Such examples can be good and bad: Hitler's economic reconstruction of Germany in the late 1930s; Mahatma Gandhi's resistance to the British Empire; Christopher Columbus' belief that the world was round, which inspired a crew (who did not share his belief) to follow his leadership.

The change-leader must be people-centred, positive and supportive of the change process. People fear change because it threatens their security, ideas, beliefs and habits, therefore leaders must offer support and help when managing their staff through the process. Part of this help and support is demonstrated by giving full participation in the planning and decision making. The change-leader must plan to impart as much information as possible to the staff and encourage them to express their feelings (both negative and positive) towards the change. Change is about developing a way of thinking and behaving. It is a set of opposing forces which we call 'restraining' and 'driving' forces.

We also analyse change in terms of communicating the power structure of the organisation in order to see who is with us and who is against us. Change is to do with decision-making processes and human relationships.

In all this, the change managers must have clear goals (short-term, tactical aims) and objectives (longer-term strategic views), which accurately reflect the priorities that have arisen and been developed from participative discussion. Change should begin at the point where people have the most control of the situation, and thereby the greatest chance of making reliable predictions (good and bad) about the outcome. Collectively, we must recognise the interdependencies of our organisational systems and the effect change can have; what appears to be a small change may create a whole new environment. As we are told in chaos theory, a butterfly flapping its wings in Peking may cause a storm over the Caribbean.

All too often we enjoy the results of change but we are not happy about going through the change process. Observing the game from the touch-line is easier than taking part. Change for the purposes of improvement and advance is a relatively new concept in historical terms; the Greek and Roman Empires strove only to maintain the status quo, and this concept influenced Europe until the close of the Middle Ages.

We know that change only works in the long term when it is made visible. We shall stress throughout this book that particular successes in the change programme must be made visible.

It is worth considering the difficulty any of us has in trying to change someone's opinion, or convince them of a belief they do not hold (convince a sceptic to believe in ghosts, for example). What is the greatest barrier? The obstacle that cannot be overcome in these situations is holding up a tangible proof that cannot be argued against. No matter how strong our religious convictions we rarely 'convert' unwilling disbelievers because there is no proof on offer. We rarely convince anyone of the existence of paranormal phenomena simply because, no matter how strong the evidence, there is no tangible proof. But when tangible proof is presented it simply cannot be argued with. By holding up the successes of change for all to see we immediately diminish the resistance to change that is based on the phrase 'I don't believe it can work'. With that barrier out of the way, many other resistances fall and the programme can move ahead.

Until recently, our education system did not prepare people for change, and our early home lives probably still do not. Most of the lessons we are taught are designed to create stability rather than enjoy change.

All too often we recommend change for other people unaware of a basic axiom of change – that any change (positive or negative) in one part of the organisation will result in spin-off effects in other parts of the organisation, which again result in a more complex and difficult implementation of the change. 'Great fleas have little fleas on their backs to bite 'em, and little fleas have lesser fleas, and so *ad infinitum* . . .'

Change is an exciting experience, and highly motivational if presented in the right manner. Life without change would be dull indeed; we cannot any longer envisage living in a world where certainty has replaced dynamic challenge. Our Roman soldier on Hadrian's Wall was asked by a friend if he thought there were any lands beyond Britain. 'No,' he replied. 'How can you be so sure?' his friend asked. 'Easy,' said the soldier, 'if there were any lands beyond Britain Rome would have built a road to them.' If that sounds quaintly naïve, consider that as recently as 1899, less than a hundred years ago, the director of the US Patent Office stated that 'Everything that can be invented has been invented'. Such certainties must have been comfortable, but they were never more than illusions. The only certainty was change.

AIMS OF THE BOOK

Organisational change has not been well documented, reflecting that many programmes for change have been 'hit-and-miss' affairs. There have been few effective guideline books on this increasingly important subject. The aims of this book are as follows:

1. To assist management in identifying the need for change   All too often change has been the response to a 'gut reaction', and has subsequently proved unnecessary or wrongly devised.

2. To structure and plan the programme for change   We now know enough about change and the effects of change on organisations and individuals to make more effective forward forecasts of outcomes. Change outcomes need not be random; this book shows how to make them controllable.

3. For those who have to implement change programmes, this book offers a sequence of practical guidelines for making the

tasks manageable   The book includes important advice on motivating others towards accepting the changes.

4. This book provides proven, workable guidelines to identifying the people who can make change happen most effectively   Putting the right team together at the beginning can save months of wasted effort.

5. For individuals who are undergoing, or are about to undergo, changes at work this book is a practical guide to what to expect, and how to respond most constructively to make the changes work for you.

Note: During this book there are references to three 'operators of change' and a definition of these will be useful to the reader from the start.

Change consultants   These are the external advisers and planners brought in to a company to assist in devising, planning and training for the change programme.

Change managers   These are the department heads who are managing change in their sections of the organisation; together with any other managers who are networking with them.

Change agents   These are carefully selected people who actually make change happen 'at the coal face'. They are chosen on the basis of their ability to lead the change programme. They become the experts in the process, and the interface between management, the change plan and the work-force. Chapter 11 is devoted to the change agents.

I

PREPARING
FOR CHANGE

1 | WHY CHANGE IS ESSENTIAL

▌CHANGE OR GO BUST!

A study of evolution shows that those races or species that are able to adapt to new environments survive; those who do not become extinct. For example, every schoolchild knows of the long and successful reign of the 'terrible lizards' – the dinosaurs. They lived for 150 million years and their history was one of continual, successful adaptation. However, most modern theories of their extinction suggest that they encountered change to which they could not adapt, probably a sudden environmental change.

The Aztecs of Mexico, an advanced and highly developed culture safe in 'the great kingdom', were aware of worked metal but continued to fight with arrows and obsidian-tipped wooden swords. Such weapons had been effective against their neighbours. However, they were of little use against the Spanish steel of Cortez and the *conquistadors*.

With the benefit of hindsight historians have always been able to establish the reasons for those great events which we call change. The challenge for modern business is to find a way to move from a reactive response to change, towards a more proactive stance. To

put it more simply, modern companies must become anticipators –
and creators – of change.

▎CHANGE IS A RESPONSE TO DEMAND

A healthy response to change means recognising that the needs and
desires of those we are dealing with have changed. We must further
recognise that in order to survive we must respond with changes of
our own.

The Industrial Revolution in Britain meant that people left the
land to work in the new factories. They needed somewhere to live so
houses were built next door to the factories. The demands of the
work-forces of the day were basic by today's standards: money and
shelter in exchange for work. As a result people lived and worked in
polluted and unsatisfactory conditions, but the needs of change
were being met by the standards of the times. In our modern society
different sets of needs have to be catered for: people now demand
good housing and less pollution, for example.

Businesses have always had to manage change, though they have
not always been successful at it. The most important change issue
facing modern companies, particularly in the Western world, has
been the move from a very stable trading environment to the unstable conditions of modern commerce. For a short time after the
Second World War most companies were able to continue trading
in very stable conditions. Sources of cheap raw materials and cheap
labour were available from the former colonies of the British
Empire, and reliable markets were under the control of most of the
large Western powers. However, with the emergence of the
independent countries which had been our traditional source of
labour and materials, we in the West lost that stability. As these
countries demanded more for their materials and manufactured
goods a new basis of trading was created; the choice was, simply, to
pay higher prices for their products and services or look elsewhere
for alternative sources of supply.

The longer-term effect of this was that companies could no longer rely upon their traditional sources of supply, nor their traditional sales outlets. Distribution routes changed due to economic and political upheaval. Companies began to form alliances and treaties with countries as well as with other organisations worldwide, in an attempt to bring some stability back into their economic sphere of influence.

Very few companies in Britain, or indeed in other countries of the industrialised world, had predicted these changes; they did not form these alliances before the Second World War.

The first response of business was to try to recreate stability

In the years of change that followed the Secord World War companies began to form into what we now call conglomerates. These collective groupings allowed companies to protect their supply lines and increase their market share in the countries where they were operating. Companies have carried out policies of vertical integration (owning the chain of purchasing and supply, from raw material extraction through production and distribution) and horizontal integration (buying out competitors).

In Western economic systems, new trading blocs are being formed, the European Community (EC) being highly visible at the present time. Facets of the EC, such as monetary union, are an attempt to bring stability into an increasingly chaotic system. Such unions are, obviously, for the benefit of the members of the club: often such benefits are to the detriment of the countries of the Third World who are not invited to join.

GATT (General Agreement on Tariff and Trade), together with subsequent Kennedy round talks and the Uruguay agreement is, however, an attempt to bring the Third World into partnership with the Western and South-east Asian trading blocs. The recent GATT talks difficulties at the end of the Bush presidency seem to have been, in part, a reflection of the 'conflict of interest' between the GATT countries and the new European union.

CUSTOMER-DRIVEN CHANGE

A vitally important, and more current, reason for change is what management consultant Tom Peters describes as the 'customer revolution'. Companies have become aware that customers are demanding a response to their needs, wants and desires. In times of recession, when the customer has less money and demands greater value for it, such an attitude becomes even more pronounced. This was not particularly the case in the past; consumers even as recently as 20 years ago had very little choice in the products and services they were being offered by companies. The most famous 'choice' ever offered to consumers is probably Henry Ford's 'Any colour [car], so long as it's black'. In the modern day, such a choice would immediately face a competition of multicoloured alternatives. Hawks would soon see the gap in the market caused by customer demand.

Because disposable incomes in the past were much less than they are now, demand could not be met by bridging the gap through imports, as the costs of importing foreign goods were prohibitive. Increased disposable incomes and a host of other changes that are examined elsewhere in this book have meant that new, higher demands can be met from imports – variety is now available.

This means that companies have had to move from a production-led philosophy ('you buy what we make') to a customer-led philosophy ('we make what you want to buy').

In most of the companies where we are working as consultants, we have seen the creation and expansion of customer focus groups, customer liaison departments and customer strategy departments. These departments study the markets, and try to anticipate the needs and wants of the customers. We have to bear in mind that the customer is now often more discerning than, say, 20 or 30 years ago: a company's product can be quickly rendered obsolete by life-style changes, or attitudes towards that particular product.

The perceptions of customers have to be accounted for; they can no longer be taken for granted, nor can they be manipulated. Jewellery boss Gerald Ratner is probably still regretting his comment in

1991 that he sold a product that was 'crap'. His jewellery group suffered enormous losses over the following year and the group's new chief executive indicated he believed that the 'crap' comment played a part in creating those losses. However, many customers moved their custom to other jewellers not bearing the Ratner name, not realising that these other shops were still part of the Ratner group. The customer showed that he or she could exert influence (even if there was a limited knowledge of the market and where to go for alternatives!).

TQM

One response to these changed conditions in larger companies, and to some extent in some smaller ones, has been the embracing of 'total quality management' (TQM) with the basic philosophy that the customer is always right. TQM demands that we meet the customer's needs by asking exactly what the customer wants. Customers' wants and needs are continuously changing, albeit in small steps. This means that a company providing goods and services must monitor these small changes and build them into their products and services, or run the risk that somebody else will enter the marketplace having identified similar needs. Often ex-employees of 'traditional' companies have done this extremely successfully and we are now beginning to see what we call the Fountain Effect.

The Fountain Effect is where innovative thinkers and creators of traditional companies, having identified the changes, leave their companies and form new, radical, smaller companies meeting the newly identified demands. These companies grow ('fountain upwards'), become bigger, often lose their radical thinking and adopt traditional thinking in their turn, and the new innovative thinkers and creators that have developed with the company leave and form a new generation of smaller companies responding to newly identified needs. The computer industry is probably the most visible example of this trend.

Such fragmentation of businesses into smaller units is now almost purely customer driven.

ENVIRONMENTAL CHANGE

Companies also face pressure for change as a result of attitudes towards the environment. With increased awareness of environmental impact upon local communities, and indeed on the whole world, companies are having to rethink the way they manufacture certain types of goods. The petrochemical industry in particular, and the chemicals industries in general, have been forced into environmental considerations. In order to retain their licences to operate, companies in these industries must – over a period of time and with the agreement of the local communities – change their working practices and their technologies so that they are not polluting the atmosphere, the rivers, farmlands and so on. In the past this has not been a particularly significant issue.

One of the change problems to address here is that customers often do not wish to pay higher prices for the goods being produced in a more environmentally friendly way. This means that the costs of environmental protection have to be assimilated by the manufacturing industries. To some extent this is forcing basic manufacturing industry to set up companies and contractual relationships abroad, particularly in the Far East. In some such locations the local 'rights' to operate are concerned with somewhat less stringent regulations; businesses there are often more economical to operate.

STAKEHOLDERS FORCE WIDER RESPONSIBILITIES

Another reason companies face change is the growing awareness of the concept of stakeholders (all those who have an interest in the long-term survival of the organisation). In the past, companies could operate virtually in isolation. Such organisations were a partnership between management, the City and the bankers, or whoever was supplying sources of finance. Even the shareholders had only a very limited say in the running of the companies they owned. However, the modern concept of stakeholders reflects a corporate recognition that companies are responsible not only to their shareholders and management, but also to the work-force, the communities in which they operate, suppliers and customers.

The problem here is that the views, needs and desires of the stakeholders are not always the same. For example, the shareholders may want to maximise dividends (which represent their income), whereas management may want to retain as much money in the business as possible in order to achieve their long-term strategic plan. The work-force may be looking for job security, improved health and safety, and good working conditions. The local community may be looking for a cleaner environment, support for the local schools and colleges, and other aspects of the local community.

When *suppliers* and *customers* are included in the definition of stakeholders, we can readily see that meeting the needs, wants, aspirations and demands of all these diverse parties makes a company a much more difficult and complex animal to manage than it has ever been before.

It is worthy of note at this point that to some extent this concept of stakeholders is still regarded as tentative. The recession of the late 1980s and early 1990s indicates that when times are hard anything can be sacrificed for profit and short-term survival – itself often a necessary response to a changing business climate.

LEGISLATIVE CHANGE

Companies must also change in order to manage, or adapt to, new legislation, some of which is coming from the EC (i.e. the Social Chapter) and some from our own parliament (i.e. the Citizen's Charter). This legislation is often brought about by public pressure as a response to accident or disaster, discovery (such as the knowledge that certain types of asbestos caused illnesses), environmental awareness or other socially desirable changes.

To date companies have usually responded to legislation

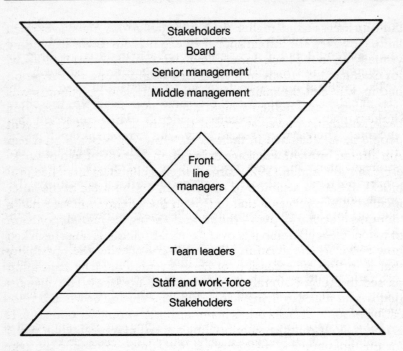

Figure 1.1
A diagram of the interactions at work in our organisations

reactively. In order to be proactive to change, companies must anticipate future legislation, and carefully monitor and consider environmental issues, work-force issues and so on. The business community must show that it can put – and keep – its own house in order, rather than be dictated to by the impact of legislation. This reactive pose can often be costly.

Change in the aviation industry

We cannot guess at any possible legislation that might occur, but a look at events in the aviation industry might offer a clue to new legislation. It is recognised that the first and last few minutes of an aircraft flight are the crucial ones. The greatest potential danger lies at these times. For this reason airports were constructed outside built-up areas so that higher-risk manoeuvres took place over open land. However, the 'urban sprawl' ended up with towns expanding virtually up to the back doors of most airports. London Heathrow, for example, is virtually in the middle of a city. For a time aviation had its way and the main concession to the new neighbours was noise abatement, reducing night flights and, when flying, cutting back on engine power at crucial times of lift-off just to prevent people being deafened in their sleep. However, a bomb on a Pan Am aircraft brought wreckage down on the Scottish town of Lockerbie in 1989, and in 1992 a cargo-carrying jumbo jet ploughed into blocks of flats in a suburb of Amsterdam. In the wake of the latter incident it was revealed that in Britain the aviation industry had a 'doomsday scenario' plan – the scenario being the mid-air collision of two passenger jumbo jets over Central London. It must be asked how seriously the aviation industry is considering the possibility that a further repercussion of these events could be legislation passed to prevent aircraft flying over built-up areas. The changes that would make to flying – including the closing down and relocating of some of the world's major airports – could be dramatic. It is not unlikely that the aviation industry has more fears than plans for this possibility. If history is a model, those who *have* thought about the problem will be ignored until legislative change is forced on the industry.

TECHNOLOGICAL CHANGE

Companies face change to take into account, and indeed use, the new technologies that are arriving in the marketplace. These new technologies, including information technology (IT), have had a great impact upon businesses. There can probably be no clearer example than the introduction of computerised printing technologies that have all but destroyed the 'conventional' printing industry. Such changes are rarely welcomed without disruption – consider the 'Wapping riots' following the move of newspaper publishers away from Fleet Street.

Certain industries, for example television, video-recording and radio industries, have found that their capital bases have been eroded because new technology has made them worthless within a short, say two-year, time frame.

New technology has obviously also had an impact on the work-force. Much of the most modern technology has outstripped the skills of the work-force and – perhaps more importantly – management's ability to train the work-force to manage it. Those that have the skills to manage such technology are a valued resource. This means that certain sections of the work-force are at a premium and can command increasingly higher salaries. Such a position often defeats the purpose of introducing the new technology in the first place, since the most common reason for changing technology is to reduce costs.

THE KNOWLEDGE WORKER

Companies also change because of the modern level of education reflected in their work-forces. There is no doubt that the modern 'knowledge workers' are more educated, more motivated and more highly trained than their predecessors. People have been brought up to expect a higher degree of job satisfaction and opportunity than in previous years.

Unfortunately, it is not always the case that management itself is more educated or more highly trained. Indeed, we can argue that very often the work-force has now outstripped management's ability to manage it. This is because management are still managing in old, traditional ways. Furthermore, some managers still have very little interface with their work-force. They are either unaware, or have chosen to ignore their awareness, of new attitudes in their staff.

PRIVATISATION

The privatisation policies of the Conservative governments since 1979 have led to enormous change in telecommunications, water supply services, utilities such as gas and electricity supply, and so on. Companies that were formerly *services* have been forced to rethink their philosophies and operate as *businesses*. The public's perception has been mixed. Many have welcomed the increased efficiencies of privatised industries, but have been disgusted with the enormous profits accrued by what amounts to government-licensed monopolies.

There have been many visible effects of these changes.

- In the electricity supply industry privatisation has meant 'productivity deals': the number of electricians employed has been reduced; there has been some erosion of sickness and holiday pay benefits; and service levels have increased with more service calls a day being made.
- In telecommunications there have been many changes that have caused public comment. Telephone boxes are now repaired nearer to within the goal of twenty-four hours, but isolated communities fear that their 'non-profitable' boxes may be withdrawn. Directory enquiries, as a free service, used to be so inefficient that if you could get them to answer at all you asked if they had been away on holiday! Now they answer immediately, but you are paying for every enquiry made. With only profit as a motive, rather than service, the telecommunications industry has been criticised for introducing the higher charge rate '0898' numbers, where there have even been allegations of making money from pornography. At the present time there are public fears that the 'emergency' service telephone lines will be privatised and that efficiency might be diminished.
- In the power generating industry privatisation has meant that the government has lost control of the buying power of raw materials with the industry free to buy coal from abroad. The effect on the British coal industry is in flux even at the time of writing.

All these changes have been fascinating. However, the change from privatised back to nationalised would be equally interesting should it occur. At the present time even the Labour opposition has accepted the privatised position, but nothing is carved in stone. A future Labour government may well decide to go down the renationalisation route, with complex consequences and involved change programmes.

THE PRICE OF FAILURE

We have said that companies must change in order to face, and challenge, their competition. More importantly these days, companies must also change to beat off predators in the marketplace. Companies that don't change lose customers to their competitors and are eventually stalked by a hawk-predator. Such companies are bought out cheaply because the City and the shareholders – who now control most of our large companies – have a different image of the company from when it was first founded. In the 1970s this resulted in famous cases of 'asset-stripping'; buying companies that were so cheap that their total market price was less than the sum of the component assets. These companies were broken up and the most valuable bits sold off, the rest discarded. Currently, the mere threat of takeover can force major changes upon even our largest organisations, as we have seen with Hanson's tentative bid for ICI.

One way or another all businesses are affected by change because the business world is dynamic. Businesses have the obligation of being either leaders of change or followers of change. Those that ignore or resist change are quickly overtaken.

Customers are seeking quality, suppliers are seeking commitment and employees are seeking recognition among their rewards. This means that companies must change the way they behave towards their stakeholders; these changes must go all the way down to the roots of the organisation.

This book explains the change programmes needed to ensure that effective change is managed in your company, to prepare you and your company for an exciting future of continuous change.

2

THE WAY WE DO THINGS NOW

In order to manage change we must first understand the culture of the organisation. The culture of any organisation is the set of values, behaviours and norms which indicate to people what to do, how to do it and what is acceptable. In other words, it is 'the way we do things around here'.

The culture of an organisation can often be recognised by the management style, i.e. how the company is run. The assumptions we make about how things should be done, and the culture and values which underpin the way we act are based on this.

Often, this culture is supported by artefact signs and symbols that display how we are operating our businesses. In a customer-driven culture we see, for example, posters displaying a huge lion ('king of the jungle') and slogans like 'the customer is king'. Another favourite of customer-driven cultures is 'customers make pay days possible'. Conversely, in a production-driven culture there may be high-profile (in one case neon, flashing) signs indicating the degree of quality control coming off the assembly line. This becomes a challenge to the work-force constantly to improve the quality, safety record and so on.

We have been surprised many times – in our work with various companies in the UK, in Europe and in America – how little is known about the culture of organisations by the management who are actually running the show.

Management, and individuals, must identify how cultures arise, and must learn more about how cultures develop, before companies can be moved from one culture to another in order to meet the challenges of change. We have given a simple definition of culture as 'the way we do things around here': such cultures evolve over time, created by the actions and attitudes of people in the organisations. These can be people whose cultural influence can be both good and bad, positive and negative.

Culture is, looking at it another way, a set of beliefs or unspoken agreements that people share about what sort of behaviour is correct and incorrect in the organisation.

How CULTURES ARISE

The question of how a culture arises in an organisation is extremely complex. It often depends upon how long the organisation has been in existence, from where it has recruited its management and workforce, and what type of leadership it has had over the years.

One of the frequent criticisms of English companies is that they are very bureaucratic. This is perhaps not too surprising; we often find that these bureaucratic types of industries have recruited people from the Civil Service or local government. These organisations are notoriously inclined towards a more bureaucratic culture, since people 'bred' in such organisations feel at ease within that type of culture.

In a similar way, many manufacturing industries place great emphasis on health and safety issues. They set up recording systems, and run committees and meetings just for that issue. This leans towards a more bureaucratic way of doing things and therefore the culture appears to be very bureaucratic. The rule is often 'check everything and then check it again and if it walks, count it'. 'Every time you make a telephone call, make sure you write a memorandum afterwards summarising the telephone call, send it to the recipient who in turn can then write a memorandum back summarising his version of the phone call, etc., etc.' Empowering cultures do not act in this inefficient way.

Some companies project their culture through a 'designer image'. Barclays Bank's business centres, for example, were designed to project a businesslike image to businesspeople, to differentiate that service from the service they offered to personal customers.

We must never underestimate the impact of particular people, or new management teams, and their ability to change the culture of an organisation. Often the reason that these people can change the culture of an organisation so quickly is because there was not a very understandable or permanent culture existing in that organisation before. A strong personality with a strong management team can capture and take over the culture of such an organisation. Therefore, a further good reason for understanding the culture of the organisation is to put in place the best culture to manage change, so that in the future these organisations will not be captured by an individual or small group of people just because they happen to sit on the board at that time.

Most companies we have worked with demonstrate what we call a 'traditional' culture and a lot of the work that we have been doing recently has been in helping companies move from this traditional culture to a more progressive culture. We would define a more progressive culture as one that is empowering rather than domineering. Promotion in a progressive culture is usually based on merit (the person most able to do the job) rather than rank (the next person in line, regardless of ability.)

Traditional cultures exhibit what might be called a 'man-and-servant' mentality, a feudal way of working that is far less common in America than the UK. The professions (law and accountancy in particular) are infested with such rigid attitudes. Progressive cultures are less dependent on 'hierarchy' and more on ability.

Delegation

The first issue to look at when identifying the culture of any organisation is the degree of sophistication in the delegation process. How do people delegate in the company, do they delegate readily, are they frightened of delegation, do they delegate downwards only? Often people are not empowered, in other words they have not got the necessary permissions or authorisations to act on their own initiative. In some cases individuals find they have to request permissions upwards through the management chain; staff wishing to travel, say, first class on a railway train, have to ask permission from their immediate line manager, and the line manager, in some cases, may have to ask permission of his or her line manager in turn.

In modern companies delegation is being replaced, or at least augmented, by support and swap. Support is given to those who have tasks to do. The question of 'finding someone to do tasks' becomes not 'Who do I have who can do this?' (delegation), but rather 'Who can support me to do this task?' (support). Swapping is a more radical alternative; individuals are asked to consider swapping tasks where they feel they are not the best person for the job, taking on a role they feel more comfortable with. As with any system it relies on trust because it can be abused – it can be a lazy person's charter if misused. In companies where we have seen swapping at its most successful it is very empowering. Tasks are handled with great efficiency.

Be effective, not just efficient

Another area which indicates the type of culture we are dealing with is the difference between organisations seeking the efficient and those seeking the effective. Often, people are rewarded in organisations, financially and by promotion, because they complete great volumes of work. This is not to argue that people should be lazy, but there is a great difference between being effective and being efficient. Being efficient is working to the rule book, being effective is challenging the working methods.

There is a difference between being busy, taking up the whole day doing something and taking some 'thinking time' to plan to do something that adds value to the organisation. We spoke to one manager who had a reputation for challenging those seeming to do nothing. He had found one of his team sitting behind a clear desk, jotting random notes on a pad. 'I asked him why he wasn't doing any work. He told me he was thinking. I told him he could do that in his own time: he was here to work.' That manager probably ran a very hard-working office, but probably not a very effective one.

Not invented here

Another old favourite is the 'not invented here' syndrome. People take the view that ideas and systems developed outside their section or department can be denied credibility. They will reject any responsibility for such ideas. 'We will not get involved and we will just allow the thing to carry on' is the usual refrain.

An example of this arose in one company where we had worked where we saw four types of personal computers – and a mixed bag of software – all doing the same jobs but in different departments. On investigation we discovered that one department had researched the question of appropriate hard and software, and had concluded that one type was right for the business. The next department that needed computerising deliberately avoided that choice, seemingly because it wanted to 'discover' or 'choose' its own tools rather than use those which others had identified. In other departments the same fiasco was played out until it became almost impossible for the company to switch material from one section to another without having to hardcopy (printout) from one system and retype into a new system.

The smothering culture

When identifying the culture of an organisation we should also look out for a smothering management culture, i.e. one that is warm, cosy and safe. This is often a patronising type of culture, encouraging people to take their problems to others to be solved, rather than encouraging individuals to 'stand on their own two feet'.

Communication

In identifying the culture of an organisation we have to consider the lines of communication within it. There are the purely vertical communications, i.e. a military style with information moving from the top down to the bottom and in some cases information moving from the middle to the top, but never across horizontal lines. Peer groups are not encouraged to talk among themselves in such companies.

Very common in companies is what we describe as 'flying desks' where people hide behind their desks and computers; they come to work, switch on their machines and stay behind them all day, apart from when popping out at lunchtime to buy a sandwich. Such individuals never walk about, never get involved in teams and never get involved with the staff. Such a traditional culture is also evidenced by conformity and safety. Risk taking is outlawed and failure punished; indeed the general approach of such an organisation is to promote people who *don't* make decisions and *don't* take risks.

Such traditional cultures are not working and many companies are spending a great deal of time, energy and money in trying to move to progressive cultures. Unfortunately, many companies still only talk about change in their traditional culture; actually they are only making superficial changes (often called 'commitment by mouth'). Management declare their view of changes in the future, but then refuse to practise the new culture themselves.

The management of change is about behavioural change to the core values; getting people to act in a certain way that they can agree to. The core values of the organisation underlie the culture of the organisation.

▌THE CORE VALUES

Core values are those standards of behaviour by which management and employees wish to conduct business transactions with themselves, their customers, suppliers and other stakeholders. The core values underpin the organisational objectives and represent a code of behaviour that is demonstrated to all levels of the organisation.

A personal examination

The following check list is recommended as the first part of the process in establishing how you conduct your day-to-day business transactions within your company.

Question 1

Does your company provide employees with clear statements of requirements, including the reasons why they are being asked to do particular tasks in a particular way? Does the company share the end vision of these requirements?

Question 2

Does your company practise professionalism in its dealings with customers, suppliers, shareholders and other stakeholders?

Question 3

Is the company open, honest and approachable in all its dealings with all its stakeholders?

Question 4

Do your managers – and you – 'walk as you talk'? In other words, do you practise what you preach or do you say one thing and do another?

Question 5

Do you recognise the contribution of your staff and are they rewarded for extra effort? Do you feel recognised and rewarded by your company?

Question 6

What steps are being taken to increase the reliability of the company's support systems so that staff – and indeed customers – can rely upon the information given to them in order that they can easily make decisions?

Question 7

Do you, and others in the company, demonstrate loyalty and commitment to customers and staff?

Question 8

Do you practise quality in all your dealings with your internal and external customers, i.e. all who receive your work or your instructions? Are you empowering your staff through mutual trust and respect, or are you just delegating in a military manner? How do you feel about the way others treat you in these respects?

It is suggested that you rank your answers on a scale of 1 to 10 in order to understand more about the core values of your organisation: 1 is the lowest score representing the absence of that core value; 10 represents the core value being in place and recognised as part of the general culture. Obviously, each individual question needs to be examined and challenged, particularly if the score is 4 or below. Such low results would identify the need to adopt those core values as part of a change programme.

Management competences

The second part of understanding the culture of the organisation is to try and evaluate the management competences. By management competences we do not mean the professional, technical and managerial skills; these are often well monitored through objectives and appraisal systems. What we mean is the self-challenge to individual managers and the management team to consider how they can openly demonstrate their commitment to the new culture. Management competences are therefore those intrinsic factors (coming from within) that affect the way we behave towards ourselves, our staff, our customers, our suppliers and other stakeholders. They are also a reflection of our beliefs concerning the business and beliefs in our own ability to demonstrate the necessary skills.

Again we suggest that you rank the following questions on a scale of 1 to 10.

Question 1

Do you understand the business you are in, its people and the industry that you serve?

Question 2

How good are you at managing change and how can you demonstrate this to other people?

Question 3

In your day-to-day business life do you create a supportive climate encouraging confidence in your staff, creativity and the taking of risk?

Question 4

Do you delegate through empowerment down the line or are you still giving and receiving instructions from up the line?

Question 5

How good are you at managing people as opposed to managing things?

Question 6

Do you recognise your staff, praise your staff and reward your staff?

Question 7

How competent is your customer focus programme?

Question 8

What is the feedback you are receiving from your customers?

Question 9

Do you live in the 'here and now' or are you always living in reflected glory?

Question 10

Do you really understand where you are in the business cycle?

Question 11

How do you rank the level of your general business skills and core competences necessary to do your job?

Question 12

How good are you at total quality management and zero defects performance?

Question 13

In your day-to-day transactions with your staff do you practise and encourage activity with passion, boldness, self-belief, perseverance, courage and self-confidence?

Question 14

How good are you at selling the services of your organisation in the marketplace?

Question 15

How do you rate your own professional excellence in your organisation?

As before, it is suggested that you rank these on a scale of 1 to 10, representing your feelings about yourself within the organisation: 1 is the lowest score representing the absence of necessary skills and attitudes; 10 represents a strong positive recognition of such skills and attitudes. Each individual question needs to be examined and challenged where the score is 4 or below. Such low results would indicate some personal improvement needed on your part to prepare you for the forthcoming changes. Where specific skills are missing we suggest that you talk to the training managers within the organisation. Training programmes associated with change projects are examined in Chapter 10.

The answers to these questions enable you and management to establish the type of culture you are living and working in. Current thinking, to which we adhere, is that businesses must move from a semi-commercial, 'traditional' style of management to a commercial, high task, high people-oriented and team working culture. In such a mode, organisations can provide a quality service in order to retain and broaden their customer base, and to make profits and sufficient rewards for the stakeholders.

3 THE WAY WE SHOULD BE DOING THINGS

In order to remain competitive or, in times of economic hardship, just to survive, every organisation must instigate *the* culture that best fits its people and their ability to make the best use of available hardware, technology, working methods and so on. The problem with existing corporate cultures, as we have seen in Chapter 2, is that they are historical and well bedded in the organisation; because of this they are very difficult to change. In our experience of change projects the organisations which are most successful in their ability to manage change are those that totally involve their employees, thereby challenging the historical trends.

Successful change has to be initiated by the people at the top; change is not a 'bottom up' process. All too often, however, management forget to involve the very people they are trying to change.

The first stage of employee participation in a change process is to involve them through workshops at the stage known as 'cultural dawn'. This is the moment, through discussion in workshops, when the workshop participants establish in outline what the present culture looks like. This is usually teased out under a few key headings on a flipchart.

The next stage is to develop – with the staff – an outline of the type of culture they would like to live in. From recent work and analysis that we have done in major UK corporations we have seen a pattern emerging. Obviously there will be specific core values applicable to different types of organisations. For example, we believe that enjoyment should be built into work, but 'fun' may be a difficult value for an undertaker to instil in his business. Likewise 'openness' may not be encouraged in MI6. However, for the most part, our commercial and manufacturing industries have similar values and are trying to shape their cultures within similar guidelines.

There will, of course, be regional and industry differences in different companies; there will also be resistance to some aspects of change because of conflicts in management style. Part of the problem arises when control of a company moves from one generation of owners to the next generation. The culture that worked well for the founding fathers may not be so suitable in a new structure.

▌RESPECT

One of the most important core values for change in the organisation is *respect* which to our mind means respect for the individual. Another is empowerment (see below).

Respect for the individual is often just a matter of good manners, treating others as we would like to be treated ourselves. Whatever the position of the individual we must recognise that they are part of an interdependent organisation, and that each has a special and important task to perform. Without their important function no task can be done with the necessary efficiency or in a desired manner. The work of many people is often taken for granted because it is designed – as a comfort factor – to be 'in the background'. However, if the work of cleaners, security guards and canteen staff is not done, then their absence becomes very intrusive. We do not admire a company's toilets, but we quickly notice them if they are not working. The importance of all members of staff should be recognised; we must give the same respect to all as we more commonly do to our peer groups and certainly our bosses.

EMPOWERMENT

'For every pair of hands we get a free brain.' The new culture recognises that management must empower its staff; in other words allow and encourage them to take maximum decisions but within the levels of authority. All too often management castrates its work-force, not letting individuals make even simple decisions. In one UK multinational where we have worked the request to travel first class on a plane had to go to the most senior executives; even first-class travel on a train was a matter of corporate grade and not of necessity.

But empowerment is much more than allowing staff to spend money. Empowerment is the realisation by both management and staff that rules are merely guidelines; very often in order to get the job done rules have to be broken, or at least bent a little. Trusting and open management, with a trained work-force, allows individuals to bend or break those rules without prior permission, and accepts occasional failure as an inevitable part of learning. Empowerment is about testing the corporate boundary rules. People must be able to stretch themselves and their confidence against rules that are historical and working only for the organisation as it used to be, not as it is now, or must be in the future.

As Rosabeth Kanter, author of *The Changemasters*, has pointed out, a manager can only get things done through other people. In order to maximise the use of people it is therefore necessary for the change manager to move from trying to control people to a position of empowering them. Though she acknowledged that rules and regulations were necessary, Kanter correctly stated that if management tries to make people do what it wants by controlling them, then employees will only use a fraction of their brain power. Such an attitude will prevent individuals from using, and developing, their full potential. It will restrict their opportunities for personal growth and development. The consequence for the organisation is that management will be failing to tap a source of future improvement which it will need to become, and remain, competitive in the marketplace.

In order to empower people there are many things that change managers can do.

- They can make clear what tasks are required from people, offering a method of approach but also allowing those people to find their own approaches.
- They can make visible the ways in which people's work adds value to the organisation.
- They must have, and communicate, a vision of the company and its future.
- They must support their staff, at both a personal and organisational level.
- A great deal of corporate work now takes place in a team environment. The duty of a team leader is not only to get the job done but also to look after the needs and wants of the team members. That includes representing them inside and outside the organisation. In this book we set out the teambuilding functions of change management; we have set out the wider guidelines for corporate teamwork in our book *Managing Your Team*.
- Management must develop the best way of doing the job. The best person to advise how to do a job is not someone reading from the firm's rule book or flowchart, neither is it a promoted manager who was doing that particular job twenty years ago. The right person must surely be the person who is here and now doing the job. That person is the local expert, and management must use that expertise, although with the input of others who have historically done the job – as advisers to the person in the here and now.

In these ways management can develop better working methods, in turn leading to the continual improvement process that alone will create the edge against competition.

Empowerment includes training, motivation and setting examples, by both staff and management. These are dealt with separately because they involve important issues in their own right.

COMMERCIAL VALUES

Commercial values in organisations mean customer focus, a wide range of 'successes' and being effectively competitive.

Customer focus

This is the awareness that the customer is the reason for the business to exist. It is extraordinary how many businesses operate almost entirely 'within'; concentrating on getting everything in the company right – and never considering the customer as a part of the business. Yet what purpose would any business have if it had no customers? In the late 1980s and into the 1990s the UK, along with most of the industrialised world, has suffered a prolonged recession. Such recessions concentrate the minds of business management on customers; in times of growth, however, management shows a lamentable tendency to leave the care of customers to public relations and advertising agencies. Customer focus means identifying the operations of the business with the customer. Businesses must 'set out their stalls' to them, showing what they want to sell, but also being responsive to customer demand.

Some organisations – through accident or legislation – find themselves in near monopoly positions. The public services such as gas, electricity, telecommunications and so on, that were privatised in the 1980s and 1990s, are good examples. In such monopoly (or near-monopoly) situations the needs of the customer are often ignored. We might also look at what the UK banking sector is having to do to retain its customers. The issue of codes of conduct and declarations of how responsive they have now become to the customer are the cornerstone of banking advertisements.

Customer focus is also understanding that customers have choices. Cultural change programmes work towards the premise that the customer really has no choice because 'we are the best'. Businesses seek continually to demonstrate this fact to customers, and their own work-forces, through work measurements and other issues that this book examines.

Success and competitiveness

Being successful and competitive is a more difficult – and often painful – issue because it recognises that we have no 'divine right' to sell, that our customers owe us nothing that we do not rightfully earn.

Commercialism in this sense is awareness of continual improvement so that the products and services that companies are supplying are not only up to date, but are also cost-competitive. This means that fast and accurate information (costings, marketplace projections and so on) not only has to be calculated by the management involved but also communicated down the line. Then all levels of the work-force can understand not just their job, but also their contribution to helping their company remain competitive in the marketplace.

▌INTEGRITY

Integrity involves honesty and constructive challenge.

Honesty

This means being open and truthful in all dealings with customers, suppliers, staff and other stakeholders. There will be times when it is necessary to be 'economical with the truth' – no one can expect a research department to give its rivals in other companies new product development secrets, for example. Also, companies sometimes cannot be fully open with people for practical reasons of security. However, honesty is still the *first weapon of influence* for the change manager. Honesty creates trust. A management's ability to be honest is based on previous experiences, attitudes and beliefs about people and organisations. Honesty takes time and considerable effort to develop; it takes a commitment from management. But open and honest cultures do exist, do win and are very commercially successful.

Constructive challenge

This means the ability not to copycat work that has gone before. People need not always agree with the organisation as just represented by the line managers. If the work-force has a set of beliefs and values that it believes in, then that is the bedrock of how people should act in an organisation. It is wrong to demand that people continually sacrifice their beliefs and values on the altar of expediency or pragmatism. From our experience, wrong-headed management force people with strong convictions just to 'keep quiet' while decisions are being made. Later, those people justify their sacrifice with expressions like, 'Well I would have liked to challenge the boss on this issue but it's more than my job's worth'. Such attitudes, forced by an outdated company culture, are unhealthy for both the organisation and for the individual.

The problem is one of weak management and lack of personal style. All too often management style is a reflection of the bosses in charge at that moment, with the up-and-coming managers just copying that management style because they see it as the path to promotion and personal development. Sadly, in such companies they are right – that *is* the path. In the professions – perhaps particularly the accountancy profession – there are very clear examples of this. Larger accountancy firms face new competition in certain areas of their work because of legislation such as the Financial Services Act. They need commercial and customer focus skills more than ever before, but competent and effective managers often stay at that level, and are not made partners, because they are not seen as coming from the same mould as the existing partners. The selection of those who will be promoted to partnership is rarely more involved than choosing someone who knows which cutlery to use for which course of the meal!

Of course, where management is effective then 'copycatting' is not of itself a problem, at least in the short term. If management is successful and suits the culture of the organisation, or indeed the new culture that change managers are trying to achieve, then use it as a model. Often, however, this is not the case. In such circumstances it is important to challenge the management style. Through workshops with senior managers, consultants (such as us) analyse how and why the present management style has arisen. We demonstrate to junior managers, and the work-force in general, that just because a company has previously acted in this or that way, and 'x' results have been achieved, that may or may not be the way they want to act in the future. Throughout this book we examine the role of consultants in this programme, but clearly an organisation's existing management can only be effectively challenged by external agents brought in as *agents provocateurs*.

QUALITY

One of the areas of change that all companies have had to accept is total quality management (TQM). It is sufficient in a book on change programmes to make clear that quality is about the mental attitude of excellence; being 'best in class' and striving for zero defects.

Excellence, at least the pursuit of excellence, is the subject of many books, training courses and company initiatives. Excellence cannot, however, take place in isolation. The total culture of the organisation must be geared to the concept that 'whatever we do we are going to do it in the best possible way'.

'Zero defects' is an easy concept to understand, but often a difficult one to introduce to work-force and management. Although 'zero defects' may be, in some people's minds, an impossible dream when demanded in society, it has virtually been achieved where the pressure to do so is great enough. In our change training and consultancy work sessions we use the example of payslips. Money is such an emotive issue with individuals that most payslips in most organisations are as near to an example of zero defects as is possible. Management cannot allow payslips to be wrong because of the extremely demotivating effect this can have, because all errors cause staff difficulty in one or another way. Where the errors leave staff with too little take-home pay the staff are quick to complain. Where the error leaves staff with too much take-home pay they may keep quiet for a number of months. However, because the Inland

Revenue have such effective checks, almost all errors are caught up with in time. Staff are then asked to repay the taxes, with further demotivating effects.

We examined the effect of this in one large company which had a considerable package of 'perks' for staff; cars and other taxable benefits. The intention was to be a generous employer, on the basis that such an attitude would create good morale. However, the company did not declare the benefits to the Inland Revenue, relying on the overriding regulation that individuals are responsible to notify the Inspectors of Taxes of their personal taxable circumstances. When it became obvious that staff had failed to do so, memos were sent out reminding the staff that they had a duty to tell the Revenue about their perks – which the staff duly did. Several hundred people were then promptly sent demands or PAYE coding adjustments costing several thousands of pounds, covering taxes underpaid for two or more years. The distress, loss of morale – and indeed trust – this caused became one of the most significant reasons for a whole training and consultancy exercise designed to change procedures and – probably more importantly – to demonstrate that change to the work-force in order to regain their confidence.

An example from the other end of the 'zero defects' spectrum is purchasing a package holiday. Often quality and zero defects are non-existent; try complaining and you face the excuse 'Well, what did you expect for the money?' While there are no alternatives, people will put up with such attitudes. But the market is then open for anyone to take a large share if they present equally good products, but with the addition of customer care, quality and zero defects. Poorly-led companies can be wiped out overnight by a radical competitor. We train companies to see those opportunities and exploit them as much as we train companies to avoid the mistakes that let the competition in. Quality, therefore, is a basic core value of any organisation that wishes to survive and make a profit.

British Airways is often held up as an example of a company that moved from being poorly regarded within the industry to an airline recognised as one of the best in the world for quality of service. This has been achieved with intensive customer care programmes.

Interestingly, British Airways was one of the first companies to take the decision that everybody within the organisation – from the contract cleaners to the chief executives – would undergo the same customer care training. This was supported by a new livery, a statement of core values and backed up by massive advertising in the media. All taken together, this had the effect of motivating all employees towards the success of 'the world's favourite airline'. This has enabled the company to increase its market share and remain in profit, when a good few other airlines have not had such happy stories to tell. It will be interesting to see the effect of the recent takeover by British Airways of an old, established airline, Dan Air.

The recent controversies surrounding British Airways' dealings with Virgin Airlines should not be allowed to cloud the fact that BA's customer care programme was highly effective and highly commendable.

CHALLENGE

A company must enjoy challenge and must certainly not regard it as an affront. Only in a challenging organisation can people accept change programmes. Challenge is about inspiring courage in every individual.

People must be free to challenge management and working methods (challenging 'the way we do things around here'), the organisation (questions such as 'Are we considering the social or ecological effects of our work?'), the systems and the kit (questions such as 'Have we got the most up-to-date equipment?'), the training ('We got the most up-to-date equipment and then no one showed us how to use it!') and any other area of constructive challenge that individuals feel the need to express. There may be guidelines to the method of challenge – no company should tolerate its staff burning down the administrative offices to protest about the company's activities – but there should be no boundaries to the scope of challenge. The wider the scope, the greater the chance of improvement and development for individuals and the company.

CREATIVITY

Companies should look for, encourage, and develop flair and imagination in the work-force at all levels. In particular many people have well thought-out ideas as to how certain tasks should be performed, but often feel they have no right to make changes or even offer alternatives.

Perhaps the person who wheels round the tea-trolley sees defects in systems within a company but would not be encouraged to voice them. Perhaps they just know that there is a more efficient way of making the tea! In a company that treats that job as 'low status', and then equates that view with 'low intelligence', those ideas would never be voiced. In companies where openness allows anyone to offer whatever they believe they have to offer, some extremely good ideas flourish.

In 1991 we were asked to develop a special training programme to assist secretaries to move into management, or at least to create more from their secretarial role than the company was offering. As background information we were given correspondences that the commissioning company (a magazine publisher) had received. One letter we have in our files was typical of many.

While minuting a meeting, I am sitting listening to all these high-flying managers mulling over their problems and arguing among themselves. I find myself becoming more and more involved in their discussion and, during the proceedings, a perfectly reasonable solution to one of the issues comes into my head. What should I do?

Dare I offer my suggestion, me, a humble secretary? I have visions of piping up, attempting to air my views only to be met with incredulous stares from everyone present, as if I had just sprouted an extra head. A more likely scenario would be that I would be completely ignored, since most people expect a secretary to be seen but not heard in the meeting situation.

Through the nature of her job, a secretary often has a wide insight into the organisation of her workplace as a whole and could provide a valuable and objective contribution to meetings. Perhaps in some forward-looking organisations, secretaries are openly invited to participate in meetings.

Other secretaries on the courses we have run have confirmed that such attitudes would be typical of many of their bosses. One told us of a meeting where there had been a long discussion of food marketing which included brainstorming as to what attracted supermarket shoppers to particular food packagings. The secretary did not get the impression that any one of the people round the room had ever wheeled a shopping trolley. Insensitively they rejected her offers (from someone who frequently wheeled a trolley round the supermarket) and instead paid a king's ransom to a firm of consultants to research the subject and tell the group exactly what she had offered months before!

Companies' managements are beginning to understand that there are complex reasons why people hold the jobs they do. It has long been recognised that there are many 'high status' jobs filled with incompetent people who had 'the right connections', but it is only recently that the opposite has been recognised. People filling 'low status' jobs often do so because of poor upbringing, leading to loss of self-esteem. They have stunted corporate development because of bad schooling or family relationships. When their creativity is teased out of them in a way they relate to, most people have hidden qualities that stretch far beyond what their employers expect. Companies that look for, and find, that potential develop not only a loyal work-force, but an energised one. There are many people who are outwardly 'idle'; slogging away at work and spending the evenings watching TV. But rare is the person who doesn't dream of greater things – tap that dream and you could benefit both the individual and the company.

CO-OPERATION

There is a simple level of co-operation which merely demands that people work together agreeably. That includes helping others, supporting colleagues, acting towards others in a way we hope they will act towards us and so on.

But there is a more complex level of co-operation that modern corporate needs demand. Many tasks are now performed in teams. Teambuilding, and team dynamics, is a subject in its own right (and the subject of our previous book *Managing Your Team*, Piatkus).

Corporate change programmes must include recognition of the need to develop effective teams for short, medium and long-term goals and tasks. Companies must recruit with an eye towards an effective team – and that does not mean recruiting one homogeneous group of people, indeed, quite the opposite is required for good team dynamics. Management must know how to motivate groups as well as individuals. And they must recognise when to break up a team and create something new, rather than let the team drag its feet finding work for itself beyond its proper, useful life.

PARTNERSHIPS

As the business world becomes more integrated with the political world in a variety of ways, so more complex 'partnerships' are formed.

There have always been partnerships between companies and their suppliers, and therefore also between companies and their customers to some degree. But today companies form partnerships with 'end-user' customers ('the person in the street') more meaningfully than before. Companies form partnerships with government in taking on social duties towards staff, for example. They form partnerships with the local community, and pressure groups have forced them to consider the needs of the immediate world around their factories and outlets. Some companies have been forced by such groups to consider a wider perspective – the world as a whole. Petrochemical industries, for example, cannot easily operate without showing and demonstrating their wider ecological concerns. At the present time it is probably true to say that such concern is more demonstrated than genuinely felt, but gradually attitude is following the habit.

Perhaps more unusually, companies are forming partnerships with their own competitors. Vertical integration can be replaced, in some circumstances, by co-operation of this kind. A simple example exists with one of our client companies where their site is adjacent to that of a competitor. Both sites produce much the same material, and both sites required a cooling tower. Neither company would have used their tower to capacity, but neither site could work without one. Rather than both build one, they agreed to build one at the point where the sites were adjacent and share the facility.

Perhaps a more complex example is the suggestion, yet to be put into effect, that petrol retailing companies should be forced to sell competitors' petrol – under the rival brand names – on each others' forecourts. This would involve a good deal of building of trust and a unique form of co-operation.

The brewing industry already faced similar demands but has so far skirted round them rather than face them. An enquiry into brewing 'monopolies' concluded that the customer would get a better overall deal if public houses were forced to sell a wider range of beers, and not just the brewer's own (in the case of 'tied' houses.) Lip-service only was paid to this recommendation with a plethora of devices set up (separate management companies, and so on) to create the illusion without the reality. A new enquiry is likely to force a more genuine response at some time in the future. (It must be said that this is a case of weak customer focus; when the customer votes with his or her feet then, and only then, will dramatic changes arise.)

However, the most radical companies at the present time are taking even established 'partnerships' further than before. Companies that have previously considered the needs of customers and therefore treated them as 'invisible' partners are now actually inviting customers on to their product development teams within the workplace. We are currently working with several companies in the computer software industry where end-users now sit on the development panels, influencing the design of interactive accountancy software and revolutionary hardware peripheries.

PROFESSIONALISM

This concept is probably better known as one of 'duty of care' towards others. The customer may be king, and his or her demands may be needs that must be met, but professionalism demands that companies see customers as partners (as mentioned above). This means telling customers where they are going wrong, where that is the case.

For example, if you visit the dentist you probably do not know what services you require, and the dentist has a duty of care to offer you the services you need. Furthermore, the dentist has a duty to point out where you are failing in your dental hygiene. Duty of care also means honesty and it should not be abused.

Many dental practitioners we have interviewed, indicated that they believed that under the restrictions of the NHS they could not maintain a desirable quality of work, nor to some degree their own desired standard of practice. As such, many dental practices are currently going through considerable change in their attempts to shake off the National Health Service. The behaviour of practitioners will become an interesting case-study over the next decade or so.

Duty of care also includes legal responsibility. This can easily be demonstrated within the professions, where it is enshrined in training from day one. If a professional person gives accountancy, or legal, advice and someone suffers loss from that advice then they may well incur a legal penalty because they have failed to exercise the duty of care that should be expected of a trained professional. The same advice from an unqualified person ('the man in the pub told me . . .') may well not incur such a penalty as that person cannot be expected to show the same duty of care.

Businesses have a duty of care to a wide range of people, from those inside the company to the world at large. Those businesses which do not act professionally, in other words those that fail to demonstrate their duty of care, will increasingly find themselves overtaken by competitors that do.

Fun

The core value which many managers have trouble coming to terms with is that of fun. Traditional management certainly used to take the view that 'fun' was the exact opposite of 'productive'. Work was a place to work, while fun was something you could have in your spare time. Because fun was traditionally seen as recreational then clearly you could not have fun at work without taking 'recreation time'.

Of the twenty-four hours in a day many are dedicated to work. On average eight hours are spent sleeping, say from 11 p.m. to 7 a.m. From 7 a.m. to 9.30 a.m. (although often cited as 'personal time') the time is used breakfasting, washing, dressing, travelling to the workplace and with the workday ahead in mind. The next eight hours, from 9.30 a.m. to 5.30 p.m., are spent at work with a very limited range of activities available in the lunch hour. From 5.30 p.m. to 6.30 p.m., on average, is time spent travelling home. Therefore, in a twenty-four hour period around four and a half hours are 'non-work', in the sense that your mind is free to contemplate other areas of interest. Weekends are not included in this and generally do represent 'personal' time (bearing in mind that some people work six-day weeks, however). But, clearly, such a small amount of time in five (or six) of the seven days of the week is not time enough for personal development or the achievement of non-work goals. Furthermore, many people argue forcefully that the stresses and strains of work leave them doing little in the evenings except dozing in front of the television getting over the day!

Many psychologists have recognised that play and fun are the most effective ways to learn, as well as the most rewarding way to live. Work should be enjoyable. Add to that the fact that individuals spend the majority of their waking life at work, as demonstrated above, then true personal development must encompass fun and play. Since it turns out (not coincidentally, we suggest) to be highly productive, companies must embrace this idea in change programmes.

In our training programmes we have always involved elements of fun, and those are the elements which ensure that trainees remember what they have learnt. As Robert Townsend, ex-chairman of Hertz, said in his book *Up the Organisation*, 'If you're not in business for fun or profit, what the hell *are* you doing . . .?'

We have always recommended that working practices involve fun, and we have seen departments become more productive because of it. In our own offices we have encouraged this and never had cause to regret it. Our own staff are free to make what changes to the working environment they feel they want or need, and to build into their work whatever elements of fun they can. If any of our staff feel they 'need a break' then they take one; go for a walk, read a book, come back to work when they feel right. We have never measured productivity by the number of hours people sit at their desks, but rather the quality and number of tasks completed. We have never felt that our staff abuse this because it is part of an open culture which includes trust given and received. In companies where such attitudes would be abused the abuse would be a reaction to other restricting attitudes that are giving offence to the work-force.

One manager told us 'If I did what you say you do I'd never see half the staff again.' We looked around his Dickensian offices, with the rules that included allotted time to go to the toilets, and we silently agreed that he probably wouldn't! However, we examined the level of productivity that was being generated by the staff 'chained to their desks' and found that it was almost as low as the general morale. Several staff admitted that they worked when someone was looking over their shoulder; when the boss was out of the room they chattered or did almost anything to avoid the tasks at hand. We were of the opinion – from experience in many enlightened office environments – that if they were encouraged to create a light and easy atmosphere, but were properly motivated to the tasks in hand, then they, and their bosses, would be the better for it.

In an ideal world people would work to live; the fact is that in the real world most people live to work. If work is to be the main activity in life, then it must also be the activity that provides for personal growth.

4 | CHANGE AND THE ORGANISATION STRUCTURE

We trained hard . . . but every time we were beginning to form up into teams, we would be reorganised. I was to learn later in life that we tend to meet any new situation by reorganising . . . and a wonderful method it can be for creating the illusion of progress while producing inefficiency and demoralisation.

PETRONIUS (died AD 66)

Petronius, working in the reign of the Roman emperor Nero, would have felt at home in many of our UK organisations because one of the most noticeable trends in our businesses is the frequency with which senior management restructure the organisation. This willingness to change the organisation chart at a drop of a hat, often justified in the name of cost-cutting and efficiency, is having a profound and disturbing effect upon employees.

In one large city organisation where we have been working there have been seven major reorganisations in one year, all apparently for the purpose of corporate progress. In these circumstances employees often – and understandably – come to the conclusion that senior management do not know what they are doing. They are perceived as spending all of their time tinkering around with organigrams (mini-organisation charts for small sections of the business) and organisation charts. Employees feel that management is not so much fine-tuning the mechanisms, but trying to figure out how they work. And in many cases, their impression is probably not totally inaccurate.

However, in the context of 'change management', such activity sometimes gives the illusion that management is doing something; fortunately for such managers the effects of such changes cannot be measured, thereby leaving them not accountable for the results. The commonly understood see-saw of 'centralisation versus decentralisation', which used to swing from one side to the other roughly every ten years, is now being replaced with biannual changes. These are justified under the guise of flexibility in order to adapt to change.

It is time for management to rethink the theories of the organisation structure to create one that has the best of the two worlds; rigid design (no more tinkering) and flexibility (to deal with a changing world).

Management must consider who, and what, is now influencing the ways organisations are being structured.

THE HISTORY AND FUNCTION OF THE ORGANISATION STRUCTURE

When businesses were first being formed in the UK in the Middle Ages the only permanent organisation structure they could observe and study was the Roman Catholic Church. The government and army at this point in history had not yet developed into a sufficiently fixed or organised structure. The Roman Catholic Church had, however, organised itself along military lines based on the Roman Legion, which was the only permanent structure they in turn were able to use as a model. We have therefore today ended up with most of our businesses and other organisations being organised along military lines. This was reinforced after the Second World War, when our military leaders were found places of work at the tops of companies, and they continued with their military thinking in their new jobs.

This classical structure is based on the following principles.

- *Span of control* Management need to know the number of people an individual can manage effectively.
- *Unity of command* A person cannot serve two masters, therefore a subordinate should only have one boss.
- *Delegated power* Power stems from the top and flows to the bottom. Someone must have ultimate authority and a clear line of authority should exist in all parts of the organisation.
- *Clear objectives* Everyone in the organisation should have clearly defined objectives that contribute to the overall corporate objectives.
- *Delegation* Tasks and authority to act should be delegated to the lowest possible level.

The main advantages of such a structure are that senior management instructions could be sent down the line and enforced, and everyone in the structure knew where they fitted in and to whom they should report. This hierarchical system served organisations well in a stable environment, but in times of turbulence (constant and speedy change) it was too rigid for flexibility and too slow to respond to changing needs. It has also proved too bureaucratic to get tasks done quickly enough to compete with organisations that had already started to change their structures. Communication is another disadvantage of this classical structure; with extended lines of communications, and the filtering of information that goes with it, objectives get muddled and managers hide behind an ever-extending rule book. In many organisations there can be eleven layers of hierarchy between the chief executive and the front-line work-force.

Obviously, many companies have been addressing this issue and reforming their structures. Robert Horton put in a series of reforms when he was chief executive of BP to reduce bureaucracy and to reduce the authority layers between himself and the work-force to just five. These types of reforms, however, have not always been successful; middle management often fight a rearguard action to resist change and maintain the status quo. There is little doubt that many chief executives and senior managers feel more comfortable working in a hierarchy where orders can be pushed down the line and away from themselves. In fact, very often, they describe themselves as benevolent dictators.

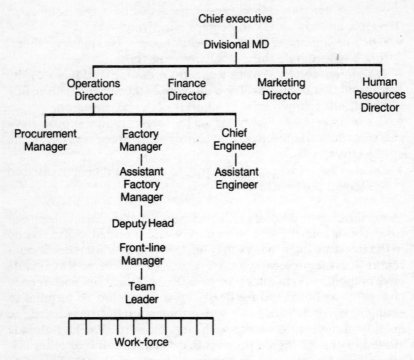

**Figure 4.1
A typical classical structure**

The example shown in Figure 4.1, extending the operations span of control, shows seven layers between the work-force and the chief executive. This classical structure is unable to deal with the strain of change and the increasing demands for more flexibility. Organisations are beginning to rethink this military style of structure for the following reasons.

Span of control is being replaced by span of communications

The traditional span of control down the line is now being replaced by restructuring organisations along communication lines.

Managers need up-to-date, fast information that is unblocked and unfiltered. People doing the job need decisions from management, irrespective of their position in the structure. An example we have seen recently is that of the environmental officer, who traditionally reported to the health and safety officer, now directly reporting to the chief executive because of the increasing importance of environmental issues.

Organisation structures are being built around information technology systems

Historically, classical organisation theory propounded that one man or woman could only effectively control six people. This was known as Graicunas's theory. Graicunas discussed the complexity of managing relationships and argued that the more individuals are added to the reporting chain the greater the number of relationships involved. He calculated that with 6 direct reports there were over 200 relationships and with 7 there were nearly 500. This meant that a manager on reaching, say, six or more direct reports would often appoint an assistant as a buffer between him or her-self and the staff and work-force. This theory has become obsolete due to information technology. Management can now, if they wish, keep in communication with as many people as they want. This can include remote offices, sites and work-stations; they can use bleepers, mobile telephones, fax machines and the more sophisticated telephone systems.

The result of this is that hard and fast rules have been abandoned. In some organisations it is not uncommon to find one-on-one relationships side by side with one-on-forty or even more. This is correctly leading management to understand that organisation structures should be designed for what is sensible for that particular business. For example, a GP doctor quite rightly operates a one-on-one relationship to do his job, whereas a junior hospital doctor may well be looking after over 100 patients. A first-line manager who traditionally would run a team of ten can now sensibly operate on a one-on-thirty/forty basis with back-up technology for resource allocations and his or her staff having personal communicators.

The impact of information technology has given managers the

facility for flexibility they need, without necessarily drastically changing the structure of the organisation. It has, however, allowed for structural change where it is needed, but could not have been implemented before. It must be remembered, however, that the benefits of information technology can often be lost as information is still filtered through the hierarchy for political and personal relationship reasons.

Businesses are now run by lower and middle management

Because of a changed business environment – with increased competition, less protection and more uncertainty – senior management have had to move to a more strategic role. The actual running of the business is now left to junior and middle management, dealing with the staff and work-force. This means that organisation structures should be built around their needs so that they can fulfil their tactical role. Organisation structures built only for the purpose of senior management cannot hope to maximise the knowledge and efforts of the rest of the enterprise. The tactical operating managers need all the information systems, back-up facilities and support structures previously only given to senior managers.

Departments of one, the so-called soloists, are on the increase

One of the outcomes of change is that more specialists are needed to service all the other parts of the business. All organisations are having to manage new legislation, new technology and new customer needs, as we have previously discussed. This has led to an increasing number of specialists who are there to serve general management, and often become a department of one (usually with a shared secretary). Usually for no better reason than vanity they manipulate themselves into direct reporting to very senior management; this leads to a very complex organisation structure – a myriad of soloists all on their own. These soloists should be brought together in teams for the function of support for the business before they become incapable of helping the very people who need their specialist skills.

There are, of course, alternatives to the classical organisation structure which can now be considered.

An empowering team structure

The first alternative to look at is an empowering structure that uses a team-based culture. Small operating teams are encompassed in a larger team. The grading structures of the organisations, and thereby the hierarchy, do not totally disappear. However, the communication lines are shortened by putting into place a larger team culture, which encourages more interaction between junior and senior graded people. The concept of empowerment is introduced and encouraged in the teams; all grades of staff and workforce are motivated to make decisions within their particular skill base and sphere of influence.

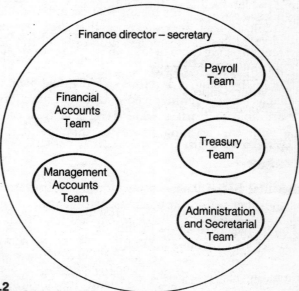

Figure 4.2
An empowering team structure

This empowered team structure creates a one-team concept that serves the needs of the business. As we have said, many grades are reflected within each circle, the grades merely reflecting ability and career progression lines. Within the whole team there is a feeling of unity of purpose, and less of hierarchy and single status.

We have been instrumental in forming and promoting empowering teams for multinational companies in the UK and USA, and from the work we have done with them we can list their advantages as follows:

- staff and work-force have greater access to senior management within their team;
- participative management and joint decision making becomes the norm, as the team meets on a regular basis;
- staff and work-force feel empowered to act on behalf of the team, thereby increasing communication lines to other such teams in the organisation;
- team members adopt a more challenging role within and without the teams, which facilitates the continuous improvement of the team and the business;
- team members feel less exposed in their skill base having team support, encouraging them to take on board new initiatives, and having the ability to take risks;
- cross-training by osmosis develops as individual team members are available for and get involved in different functional areas. People are able to learn a wider level and type of skills, in keeping with the learning processes that are part of non-corporate life.

A facilitating structure

The second alternative to consider is a facilitating structure, which enables line managers to act as facilitators for the staff and work-force. In order to maximise flexibility at all levels of operation, management make themselves available for consultation and decision-making processes as and when they are needed. This means that management operate between the strategic and tactical roles as determined by the needs of the business. This, in turn, leads to the skills of management being truly mixed with the skills of the people actually doing the job 'at the coal-face'.

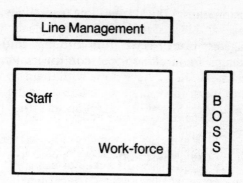

Figure 4.3
A facilitating structure

This concept identifies the staff and the work-force as a homogeneous block who have the necessary training and skills, and systems and equipment to do the job. Line management are identified as a united team of specialists whose task is to facilitate, or develop, the ability of staff and work-force to do the job. This is done through planning, problem solving, resource procurement, as well as giving leadership, coaching and positive motivation. The boss is identified as being accessible to both line management, and the staff and work-force. Like the stated position of the prime minister, the boss becomes 'first among equals' rather than a line dictator. Obviously, many of the traditional roles of management remain in place, i.e. staff assessments, promotion, discipline, communication of objectives etc., while at the operational level the structure looks less like an army (military structure) and more like an orchestra (in concert).

The advantages of a facilitating structure are as follows.

- It creates a more accessible and visible line management who become experts and tutors to the functional teams.
- Communication lines are greatly reduced.
- The boss is perceived to be independent of the staff, work-force and line management, but owing a duty to all.
- The staff and work-force can determine the tactical support they

need while working to known key objectives and agreed deliverables.

- Line management are freed from the day-to-day decision-making processes and can concentrate their energies on more strategic tasks.
- The staff and work-force have access to a greater range of line managers, and therefore skills to call upon, rather than the rigid military system.
- Line management are able to develop and increase their skill base by having the opportunity to work with a greater number and variety of teams.
- The decision-making process is eased as more collective and participatory decisions are made.
- The organisation becomes more entrepreneurial as risk moves from individual managers and teams to the more collective system.
- Demarcation, and self-protection, declines as people see the synergy in corporate team effort.
- The structure is less bureaucratic as middle men or women are either made redundant or assimilated into the operational teams.

As in all change situations there can be resistance to this type of structure. From our observation most of the basis of resistance by line management is due to habit, perceived loss of authority and fears for adequate time management. Managers who like to be very busy – often with wall-to-wall meetings – find it very difficult to free up their time to get involved with the functional working teams in the front line. However, with training and commitment, and support from the boss, most line managers see the sense, if not the urgency, of adopting such a structure.

The challenge of the younger knowledge worker upon the structure of the organisation

The old ways of organising people into structures may well be suitable to the older, traditional staff, management and work-force, many of whom may be nearing retirement. They trained and were developed in the business feudal system. They understood the hierarchy and the bureaucracy, even though they may constantly moan about them. They practise 'them and us attitudes', and defend demarcation and job preservation. They are not used to challenging the system, and are frightened to step out of line.

By contrast, the younger knowledge worker, who has more often than not been taught to operate in a team culture, is finding it increasingly difficult to operate in the old culture and organisation structures. Better educated, more worldly and better informed, the younger knowledge worker is impatient to get things done and to operate with success the skills they have been taught. Increasingly frustrated by the hierarchy, they either challenge the system until defeated and leave the organisation, or they literally die on the job. This movement towards corporate liberation is only temporally arrested in times of job shortages due to recessions. At those times feelings of pent-up frustration are suppressed until the economy and the job market picks up. The young and the fit will then move to more progressive organisations as reflected by their organisation structures. Therefore, periods of enforced employment stability should be seen as an opportunity to change the structure of our organisations fundamentally.

HOW TO IDENTIFY THE STRUCTURE YOU ARE WORKING IN

Here are five key identifiers of your corporate structure.

A classical structure

- Are there six or more layers between the chief executive and the work-force?
- Do management have military-sounding job titles (i.e. chief engineer, training superintendent)?
- Are lines of communication formal (i.e. communicated one layer at a time)?
- Can you recognise grades of staff through dress codes (i.e. the bosses wear suits, the supervisors wear white overalls, the work-force wear blue overalls)?

- Do requests for information or resources need detailed, formal requisition slips?

An empowering team structure

- Can you identify cohesive teams within departments?
- Can you and your team make decisions within general authorisations?
- Does the organisation laugh at small failures and reward success?
- Are people encouraged to feel that they 'own' their jobs?
- Are decisions made collectively (and not passed down from the top)?

A facilitating structure

- Are management seen as a support for the work-force rather than as a governing body?
- Is the boss seen as equally accessible to both line management and staff?
- Do staff and work-force regard themselves as being in the same teams?
- Are line management relieved from simple decision making? Are staff and work-force involved in higher-level decision making?
- Can the organisation flex its resources to meet any situation or problem?

5 | *THERE WILL BE RESISTANCE TO CHANGE*

One of the paradoxes of society is the development of children who are so receptive to change, even eager for it, into adults who are conservative and resist change at every level when they are at work.

We can assume with some degree of confidence that the problem lies in the way we run, or structure, our organisations. Something in our business environment must be affecting the natural curiosity of our work-forces, making people afraid to experiment, when experimentation is at the heart of all true learning.

In this chapter we will examine why people resist change and what the organisation can do to encourage change in the individual and in corporate teams.

People's resistance to change is due to their history, culture, attitudes and beliefs. Let us first examine these in the context of change, while appreciating that these issues also impact upon other parts of the organisation, such as communications.

HISTORY

The history of most organisations does not allow the general work-force and front-line managers to encourage or accept change. Most directors of major organisations are perceived to be short term and opportunist.

Some management, quite frankly, have little other ambition than to survive for a short time, maximise their earnings and protect their pension rights. If possible, they use the time to create for themselves watertight contracts of employment, so in the event of corporate failure, and redundancy, they are rewarded for their incompetence by a significant financial payoff. This is usually sufficient to upset the stakeholders; occasionally it is so blatant as to become headline news.

Particularly in times of recession, but actually most of the time whether in recession or not, most organisations cut costs by reducing their work-forces in the name of productivity. At the same time many of those companies are building new factories and distribution depots overseas, or they are forming partnerships and alliances worldwide that are very often in direct competition with their UK operation.

The resilience of staff in organisations like these has been remarkable. Over the past twenty years management have asked for that last push forward to save the comany site, factory etc.; the work-force have delivered the goods only to find that their reward has been pay freezes, redundancy and relocation. Is it any wonder, then, that staff become resistant to change and have no faith in the ability of management to deliver the promises that are supposed to be the incentives to accept change projects?

In the last quarter of 1992 the British government announced that it would close thirty-one out of around fifty remaining deep-shaft coal mines in the UK, directly laying off thirty thousand of the work-force and decimating one of the country's most traditional industries. The miners affected will have felt a plethora of emotions at such an announcement, but none so deep presumably as the emotion of betrayal. They were a work-force that had been asked to endure a great deal of change (i.e. new working methods, new technology and redundancies), and their reward was rejection. Whatever the perceived economic or other reasons why the closures should take place, the way the announcements were made public was a public relations fiasco. Certainly the off-hand way the work-force were first informed of their fate (mostly directly through the media) and the apparently off-hand way it was decided (a small cabinet group on the telephone) was not calculated to allay the inevitable resistance to such a move. Within days there was the spectacle of the government in disarray and backtracking. Whatever the eventual outcome (still in flux at the time of writing), it is difficult to imagine that those workers, when relocated into other jobs, will easily trust their future managements and governments again.

CULTURE

The culture of the West, as we have argued, has not traditionally been conducive to change. However, it is possible that society could now be making a U-turn. The modern generation appears to be more mobile, and less resistant to moving to, and working in Europe or elsewhere. This has been partly the result of changing attitudes (*Auf Wiedersehen, Pet!*) and partly due to the relaxation of rules concerning work permits and the coming of the Single European Market.

That said, it is still possible to see young entrants into companies who seek the very traditional culture of 'job for life', job security and so on. Such attitudes are those which also lead to fear of risk-taking, avoidance of challenge and so on. Getting back to Victorian values, as former prime minister Margaret Thatcher advocated, is not an attitude conducive to accepting change; the one thing that characterised the Victorian era was the search for – and for a time the achievement of – stability. When we were working in the US it was refreshing to observe a different culture, where mobility and risk were encouraged as part of personal development.

As Tom Peters pointed out in the Dillons lecture in London in November 1992, Silicon Valley in California is predominantly made up of small companies founded by young entrepreneurial and mobile people who started work with companies like IBM and AppleMac, but who became frustrated with the corporate culture and the restrictions inherent in such business systems. It must be noted that IBM is now on record as stating that it is presently implementing a fundamental shake-up of its business practices and culture. For example, it is expected that the children's games computer market will be significantly changed by IBM's entry into that field.

Companies in the UK are beginning to understand this 'culture barrier' and deal with it. Management are increasingly being heard to say things like: 'In order to remain competititve and grow our business we must get the culture right.'

For many years the Japanese have been held up as having a culture of efficiency, hard work and achievement. However, as Japanese businesses set up in the UK, we see that where the UK culture is mixed with this Japanese working style the British work-force can achieve productivity equal to, if not better than, any other work-force in the world. For example, Japanese car manufacturers in both Sunderland and Wales decided to build green-field sites and recruit a work-force predominantly under the age of thirty, led by supervisors and team leaders who were trained in Japan. This mixture of Japanese technology and management style, together with highly skilled English and Welsh work-forces and single union agreements, have led in some cases to productivity outstripping that of the car factories around Tokyo.

ATTITUDES

The attitudes that prevail in our society do not necessarily cause resistance to change. Even so, attitudes must be made more visible and discussed openly to see where they can enhance the organisation, as opposed to blocking its progress. Attitudes are formed at a very early age and are taught by parents and relatives, i.e. close contact people, in the first instance, and are later reinforced through our schooling by the books, literature and discussions to which we are exposed.

We know that attitudes are traditional in so far as they are built on history. A young adult is not necessarily racist, ageist, sexist or any other '-ist', but these 'bad' attitudes are taught at a young age and handed down from generation to generation. In our experience, with work-forces and front-line managers, the attitudes of close contact people ultimately override 'politically correct' conditioning; attitudes become firmly set at an early age.

We see that young adults entering into an organisation quickly learn the history and attitudes of that organisation, even though by then they may be obsolete and no longer applicable to that particular business. From recent work that we have been doing in the City of London, as consultants and trainers, we have observed – and been part of – a traditional culture that in all probability has little bearing now on the way that business should be run in a modern financial services capital.

BELIEFS

People's beliefs are difficult to establish. People adopt very shallow beliefs in order to work in many organisations. It takes a great deal of work – facilitated through discussion in work groups and brainstorming – for people to understand and recognise that their true beliefs are really deeper, and more complex. Often, they discover that their true beliefs are at odds with the beliefs they have been forced to adopt. People's deeper, true beliefs are determined by their experiences and what they have been taught by parents, schools and colleges. Their more 'adopted' beliefs are reinforced by peer group pressure in their organisations.

In order to manage change it is essential that change managers understand what is 'precious' to the individual. These beliefs are often hidden, although we know that they do have a substantial effect upon behaviour.

An organisation demonstrates its beliefs in its 'mottos'. Some of our older institutions have such mottos as 'my word is my bond' (London Stock Exchange), 'never knowingly undersold' (John Lewis Partnership), 'pile it high and sell it cheap' (Tesco) etc.; all phrases which very successfully abbreviated what the original founders thought their business should represent.

If we look at some of our newer organisations the corporate motto seems to be 'bottom line profits or bust'; not exactly visionary mottos likely to enthuse people. Alan Sugar of Amstrad made 'we make money' something of a corporate vision for the 1980s, but has perhaps found that 1980s success short lived. The change manager will need to establish the beliefs of the organisation or adopt the current range of 'acceptable' general beliefs, i.e. total quality management, customer focus etc. In truth these are more statements of intent than deep-seated beliefs.

It is encouraging to see that if real beliefs are missing, at least the vision and mission statements are now being augmented by clear, achievable and genuinely understood departmental objectives that are in concert with organisational goals.

Beliefs should only be made visible where the change manager has identified that the beliefs of the organisation are in conflict with the general beliefs of the work-force. In that instance making this conflict visible and confronting it is the only honest way to present a change programme.

We often perceive these conflicts. We hear sayings like 'dog eat dog' and 'let the best man win', yet we actually spend much of our time protecting the weak in our organisations.

Ultimately, committed people with strong, viable beliefs will have an input upon the work-place and eventually change the beliefs of the organisation.

THE CORE ISSUES

There are also core issues which cause people to fear change: fear of the unknown, mistrust and ignorance.

Fear of the unknown

All change represents the unknown. That alone should not be a reason for fear. All the evidence suggests that we actually love the unknown. The culture of science fiction has grown up on a love of the unknown. The unknown excites the imagination; people fanta-sise about their part in challenging the unknown. Indeed, through science fiction people vicariously 'travel to the stars', 'meet' people from other worlds and so on. Of course, vicarious adventures allow such excitements to be safe.

The problem of fear of the unknown can be demonstrated in this example; the reason such radical ideas as space travel are accept-able is that the world we dream we might live in can be adapted to accommodate us (it is our fantasy after all). The real world, how-ever, is not thought to be so accommodating. We may be ready for change but the change may not allow us to live in the world we have to face. For example, we might not fear redundancy because we love work and are afraid to lose it, but because redundancy would prevent us paying the mortgage and threaten the roof over our heads. In a fantasy these considerations could be ignored, in reality they cannot.

In order to facilitate change we must move from the unknown to the known. What is known to senior management, i.e. what can be calculated, is often unknown to the work-force. This is only because we cannot be bothered to explain to the work-force how we have planned for, and perhaps moved from, the unknown to the known. Management often fail to make clear what assumptions they have made along that path. Management often act as if the change process is of no concern to the work-force. It is, of course, an extremely bad trait of leadership to assume that, because we know what we are doing, and because of our position in the organisation, the work-force has no right to share in our thinking processes. Managers may have had to face their own resistance to change, their own fears and trepidations; to share that with the work-force would not only ease the path towards the change, but would also build a team mentality of 'we're all in this together', replacing the image of 'them and us'.

The modern knowledge worker has a right to an explanation of what management are doing, and a right to know how they got to this position. To use one of the favourite clichés of the training room; moving from the unknown to the known is a journey not a destination. Where we have led change projects ourselves we have always given clear explanations of what we are doing, why we are doing it and how we hope to facilitate the change. This honesty is most often accepted by the work-force and lessens the resultant, in some cases inevitable, resistance.

In fact, most change projects do not involve true unknowns, but they can often appear to do so. Mastering new technology or understanding organisational restructure in new markets is often just a matter of analysis, dividing the change into simple, 'bite-sized' chunks, and then explaining them. Most change projects are huge when considered as a whole, but they are implemented in small changes, and they are best presented and understood that way. New situations do arise, of course, but it is possible to apply the same thinking processes and rules of logic to any eventuality.

Ignorance

This is a difficult issue in business, because it is again based on assumptions that are both historical and cultural. There is an idea still prevalent among some senior managers that their work-force and front-line managers are either ignorant or do not have the same intelligence, thinking processes or education as they do. In fact, where there is ignorance it is generally the fault of management. Management do not explain 'the big picture' because they feel, on the one hand, that the work-force is not intelligent enough to understand and, on the other hand, that if they did understand they would not know how to handle the information they are being given. This is a challenge to the change manager; total openness is very difficult to achieve. And like anything else, it does not always work out as you hoped.

For example, in a very large multinational organisation where we were working, which was coming to terms with a new culture of openness, the company announced the sale of one of its subsidiary companies. The announcement was made to both management and work-force on the same day. Unfortunately, the sale fell through. After letting the management and the work-force believe that their company had been sold, some months later the senior management of the holding company had to disclose that the sale had now been aborted and the status quo would be maintained. The effect on the work-force was twofold. Initially the employees were glad to know of the sale and the possible effect upon them; however the with-drawal of the sale left the work-force in a state of uncertainty they had not had prior to the announcement. Now they knew they were going to be sold off when the next willing buyer came along, but they did not know when, or what the new conditions might be after that sale.

Management was in a no-win situation. By saying nothing (and not quashing the inevitable rumours that had been running around the site) the management would have been accused of not being open and honest. But by going public before the contract was finalised, management were left embarrassed, and with a demoti-vated work-force to manage.

We believe the problem was that the company was not open enough. Presumably management did not think that the employees would respond well to an announcement that there were plans for a sale, but that they had not been finalised. True, such an announcement would have left some uncertainties, but some uncertainties could not be avoided in the situation. And it would have been truthful, would have quashed the wilder rumours run-ning though the company and would not have led to the eventual lack of confidence with which management was viewed thereafter.

Mistrust

There is a tradition of mistrust between management and work-force in industry and commerce. It is built on experience for the most part; the bad management of situations by people poorly trained in dealing with other people. In some extreme cases it is the product of managements who care very little for their employees.

The history of mistrust exhibits what is known as the 'ratchet phenomenon', likened to the mechanism of a ratchet screwdriver. Every turn in one direction (bad management) reinforces deep-seated beliefs such as 'you can never trust the bosses', whereas every turn in the opposite, more positive direction does *not* weaken the reinforcement, it is simply ignored (the ratchet tightens in only one direction).

The only way to reverse the ratchet phenomenon is to have a long and strong history of trust. Then, each further example of trust will tighten the ratchet in that direction. But trust cannot be 'created', it simply has to evolve. By demonstrating genuine openness and honesty for a long period of time, trust will eventually follow. It will probably be the last such barrier to fall, but when trust is truly established it will be hard to lose. Unfortunately, no matter how trustworthy a company may be, there are always likely to be demonstrations of betrayal in other companies to which the sceptical can point and say 'maybe that could happen here'.

At the present time, for every manager genuinely committed to open and honest change, there is another who could be summed up by the following saying: 'Honesty, integrity and trustworthiness are the three most important qualities in a manager; if you can fake all three you've got it made!'

Education and background

The pattern of learning in our early lives, our schools and universities has not always been conducive to the attitudes we want in our employees. A young child is subjected to a fierce learning curve; in a relatively short space of time human children learn a highly complex amount of information. They do so in early life through interaction with others, and the environment around them. The earliest learning is experimentational; a child eats an item of food and finds it pleasant, the same child may touch a hot radiator and find it unpleasant. Based on what has been learnt the child will seek more of the food, and avoid touching radiators.

At play school or nursery this style of proactive, experimentational learning continues. Children are not 'formally' taught about three-dimensional images but they are left to create them for themselves from highly coloured, attractive, plastic building blocks.

In the past the method of teaching seven to eighteen year olds has been one of passive listening or learning by rote. If you are over the age of thirty you will remember sitting in class listening to the teacher 'explain' subjects, and many will remember reciting their 'times tables'. Certainly, many subjects were taught with academic fervour and not the slightest reference to application. Most people can remember at least one subject that they still know well today, but for which they have never found a relevance since leaving school. Indeed, most mathematics turns out to be very useful in the business world, but it can come as a surprise to discover that the practical training we get in our companies turns out to be the same thing we learnt in theory in school.

Fortunately, schoolchildren are now taught to be more proactive in learning, and to learn by application rather than rote. In effect they are not being taught, they are being trained to learn for themselves. In colleges and universities, more proactive learning has always been encouraged; personal research augmenting lectures and other direct teaching. However, senior management are only just beginning to take this training into account.

From birth to the day we start work we are basically taught proactively; encouraged to experiment with the environment around us and to learn for ourselves. Then, on the day we start work we are told 'sit there, do that'. We are told to learn by listening to those who have done the job before, we are given a rule book and told to learn it by rote. Learning becomes a passive experience; experimentation is outlawed as 'costly', 'not productive', 'risky' and is given a host of other critical descriptions.

Our demand is for the young adult to be totally passive, i.e. to do a certain job, normally of a repetitive and routine nature, and to adhere to the rules of the organisation etc. The culture of most organisations demands passivity and compliance. It does not encourage the young adult to be part of the development of the work process, or to get involved and positively contribute.

Even with a simple task ('making the tea', to use the simplest example) we should not be saying to the new recruit, 'This is the teapot, this is the kettle and this is the person who used to do the job – he or she will tell you how to do it'. What we should be saying is 'Here is the teapot, this is the kettle. Do it your way, but remember you can call on the support of the person who last did the job for advice.' Either way we end up with at least as good a method of making the tea as we had when the last person had the job, but only in the second example do we have the possibility of a new, fresh, unbiased mind creating a whole new way of making the tea that no one in the company had previously thought of.

Our above example demonstrates another area of human development; encouraging people to move from a relatively dependent state to an independent state. In a family situation, the young adult starts by being totally reliant on the family unit for support and training, but develops to the point where he or she can form their own family unit. In many ways business is similar to the family unit, but it works in reverse, and against all common sense. Just as the individual is equipped for independence, we put him or her into a framework of total dependence. Imagine a situation where as teenagers we were encouraged to live alone, find our own way in the world and so on, only to be forced to move back with our parents when we had spouses and children of our own in order that our parents could dictate the rules for our lives.

Companies take on the role of surrogate father or mother, demanding adherence to rules, regulations, rewards and recognition systems. They 'give' perks, such as career progression, company cars and pension schemes, all encouraging dependence upon the organisation just at the point when free independence is what the young adult needs if he or she is to help 'grow' the company.

The focus of our corporate education is wrong-headed

In life, and early education, we demonstrate that we are capable of learning a complex array of skills. We learn quickly to walk, talk, adapt to our immediate environment, play sports, grasp complex patterns such as chess and crossword puzzles, and understand about subjects as varied as economics, history, geography, knitting, languages. We interact at a bewildering number of levels; socially, sexually, platonically, in the company situation, in sports teams and so on. We learn basic survival; cooking, cleaning and so on. We learn higher level appreciations; religion, philosophy. And we demonstrate that we can hold all of these skills at one time, using them when they are needed, often employing several levels of thought and complexity at once.

Yet in business we are taught immediately to specialise, to focus on one skill or range of complexity. Then management are surprised that our work-place fails to enthuse or inspire us. They are disappointed that the creative spark that was so apparent on our CVs is not sparking while we are at our desks.

If the organisation then demands a very quick increase in the skill base we have developed for work, the ability to translate our natural learning abilities to our work environment is long buried and forgotten. It becomes increasingly difficult for the young adult to apply creative talents within their organisation. Quite simply, work has become an environment where a new set of learning rules has been developed, and the old ones cannot be made relevant. The training needed to make it relevant can be a long process.

Unfortunately, managers often still do not know what the skill bases of their staff are, and only pick out or try to rediscover such skills as reflect the way they are running the business at that particular point of time.

The 'goal focus' of our companies is wrong-headed

As children and young adults we live in a world of short-term time periods and short-term, achievable goals; i.e. summer term, winter term, sports days, exams, GCSEs, driving tests and so on. Having a clear objective and 'going for it' is achievable, satisfying and natural. Certainly we are capable of seeing the perspective of these short-term views within a longer term objective – the life we see ahead for ourselves. In work, however, we have been asking people to see the long-term objective only (i.e. 'here is a job for life', 'this is your planned career progression from day one to retirement' and so on). There has not, at least until recently, been any acknowledgement that people need, and need to know, their short-term, achievable goals.

Businesses have always had to live in short-term perspectives of course; one-month plans, quarterly accounts and so on. It is only recently that people have been encouraged to 'own' those goals and understand their perspective within the organisation. In the past getting out the monthly figures was merely 'the job'; what it actually did for the company was a complete mystery.

Governments in the West, operating under what amounts to a single 'opposition' system – such as America and Britain – suffer from the same problems. They make no long-term plans because they never view their term in office longer than the four or five years until the next election. During that four or five-year period they seem sometimes to be more concerned with getting the cycle of events right to bring them to a favourable position for the next election, rather than laying down longer term, perhaps more lasting, plans. It was even suggested by elements of the tabloid press that the Conservative government during 1992 might deliberately seek to stall the recovery from the recession in order that it could arise nearer to the next election! If such allegations of Western governments were true (and we are not supporting or refuting such views), then American President Bush would find it ironic that he left office just as recovery was beginning. From our point of view it was encouraging to see that President Clinton was elected to office on the basis of one word more than any other – change!

Our attitude to authority is wrong-headed

Young adults are always in a subordinate position in the family unit and at school; indeed some schools still have prefectorial or monitor systems. Young adults quite rightly look forward to the day when they will be equal to the people they have to deal with in their immediate environment. They seek a position of authority, such as foreman, supervisor etc. But most of the work-force remain – for most of their working lives at least – in subordinate positions, taking orders from others. Work-forces often regress into becoming very submissive and can only relate to management through their organised representatives. They are passive, often alienated, very bored and for these reasons it is increasingly difficult for them to adopt or see the sense of change projects. Until we successfully replace hierarchy with flatter, supportive structures designed to encourage personal growth, this will continue.

Planned change is usually initiated to find a way in which the organisation can function more effectively, utilising new information and resources. In order to introduce change so that it comes about easily, managers must take great pains to develop the appropriate behaviour in their staff so that they can continue to be effective and innovative.

The general attitudes examined in this chapter make change projects more difficult to implement; by the time people are being asked to accept a programme designed to enable them to enhance their own jobs, 'own' their own jobs and create something new in their own jobs, they have already had proactivity knocked out of them.

Guidelines

Here are some guidelines which are useful for managements wishing to initiate change.

1. The attitude of the team leader is more critical than the change itself. He or she must be people-centred, positive and supportive.
2. People fear change for the reasons stated; mostly because it threatens, or seems to threaten, their security. Support and help are needed at all levels of the change process.
3. Real participation in the decision-making process by those affected helps the progress of change.
4. Plan to impart as much information as possible to subordinates and help them to express their feelings towards the change.
5. One of the important things a manager can do in anticipating a change is to analyse the forces involved. There is a technique called 'force-field' analysis to do this (see Chapter 6 for further details). Visualise this as a tug of war where both sides are essentially even. Until some imbalance is created and either side pulls the change is not likely to begin. This can be done in three ways.
   (a) You can increase the number or strength of the driving forces. The risk here is that when the pressure is eventually lessened back-sliding may occur. Also, increased pressure often strengthens resistance.
   (b) You may decrease the number and strength of the restraining forces. In organisational settings this can frequently be accomplished through increased staff participation in the planning and problem-solving process.
   (c) You can combine the first two methods, making each more effective.

As leaders and managers you must do the following to bring about effective change.

- Develop a way of thinking about change that concentrates on the dynamics of the situation. This may reflect communications, the power structure, decision making or human relations.
- Have clear goals which reflect your priorities.
- Begin change to the point where your people will have the most control and where they can make reliable predictions about the outcomes.
- Recognise that change in any one part of the system or organisation affects the whole business. What appears to be a small change may create a totally new environment in the long term.

Also, ask yourself where to begin to plan change. Ask yourself these questions when planning for change.

1. What requires change – and why?
2. What are my motives for initiating the change?
3. What are the resources available to assist the change effort?
4. Have I made clear to those affected the purpose and extent of the change?
5. Have I made it possible for people to express objections openly?
6. How can I involve those affected in planning the change?
7. Once the change has begun, what do I need to stabilise and maintain it?
8. What are the reasons others may support or resist the change? These are the driving and restraining forces mentioned above. In the work-place we might find the following general forces; though specific change projects will have specific forces of their own.

Possible driving forces for change at work
(a) more money
(b) more interest in work
(c) reduction of rework
(d) increased responsibility
(e) higher status
(f) increased job security

Possible restraining forces for change at work
(a) less opportunity for overtime
(b) less use of skills in the new working methods

(c) less personal involvement
(d) loss of colleagues from relocation or redundancy
(e) loss of familiar surroundings
(f) fewer promotion prospects

We can then see that for every driving force there is often an appropriate or opposite restraining force, and the sum total of the 'for' and 'against' weightings are a useful tool in the problem-solving process. This is a fundamental part of preparing for change and will be examined in full in Chapter 6.

6 | MEASURING RESISTANCE TO CHANGE

The amount of resistance to proposed change is quantified, as much as that is possible, by force-field analysis.

It is said that people must see a problem as their own before they can be motivated to make changes. A good example is the story of the corporate executive learning to improve his golf swing which – he always maintained afterwards – gave him a role model for corporate change attitudes. He had wanted to improve his swing, to avoid hooking and slicing, and get longer drives from the tee. The club professional told him constantly that there was too much movement in his legs. He agreed, teed up the ball and hit the same swing as he always did. 'There's still too much movement in your legs,' the professional said. 'But I kept them more rigid that time,' he protested. 'No, you didn't,' argued the pro. This went on for a long time, and he had several expensive lessons.

Eventually the professional tried a new tactic; he turned up at the lesson with a video camera and set it up to record the swing. Several balls were 'thwacked' off the tee with great gusto by the executive, who maintained that he was keeping his legs steadier. Then he watched the video replay. 'Good God,' he said. 'I had no idea it was that bad.' He watched intently for a while, saw which areas of his body were causing the improper movements, and went back to the tee. He swore that the professional maintained that his leg positions and movements were permanently improved from that moment on.

The executive maintained that although he knew that the professional had been telling him the truth he had not been able to translate it into action until he saw it for himself.

From that time on, whenever he wanted even minor changes in his organisation he would find a way to make the problem and the desired outcome visible to his staff, and find a way to make them appreciate the benefits of each change he wanted to implement personally.

In the same way, force-field analysis makes visible, by means of a diagram, the restraining and driving forces for change. The underlying suggestion is that for every action (state or attitude) there is an equal and opposite reaction (state or attitude). These opposing forces are in a state of equilibrium. To make changes it is necessary to lessen the restraining forces against change and increase the driving forces towards change. The new balance is then at a 'shifted' (changed) position.

The best way to obtain the information to insert into the force-field analysis diagram (examples which will be shown later in the chapter) is to hold brainstorming sessions, where those involved in the change programme 'free think' through the problem at hand. Each individual may offer any suggestion; there may be no criticism, praise or comment (even by body language). At a later time there will be 'hitchhiking', where one person picks up on the ideas of another, gradually reaching solutions. In this case, the proposition is stated and then every individual is asked to offer a driving or restraining force for the equation.

Let us take the proposition of 'relocating the offices from London to Edinburgh'. What are the driving forces? What are the restraining forces?

Firstly, there are often several propositions in such questions and those implementing changes must take care to identify the components separately. Failure to do so leads to a real lack of understanding as to why the change programme is being resisted. What in fact happens is that people may well be persuaded about the benefits of change as you see it, but are resisting the elements you have overlooked, or not considered relevant.

In our example there are actually two proposals:

1. to relocate the offices from London to Edinburgh;
2. to relocate individual staff members from London to Edinburgh.

Thinking about the offices the force-field chart could look like this.

OFFICE MOVE FORCE-FIELD ANALYSIS	
DRIVING FORCES	*RESTRAINING FORCES*
(a) Cheaper rent and rates	
(b) Government grants	
	(c) Restrictive regulations apply
(d) State of the art offices	
	(e) Costs of fitting out
	(f) Costs of moving
(g) Cheaper staff costs locally	
	(h) Smaller pool of available staff
(i) Automatically losing (unwanted) staff	
	(j) Losing good (wanted) staff
(k) Losing the problems of the M25 for our delivery vehicles	
	(l) Less centralised road and rail links
(m) New markets	
	(n) Effect on existing customers
(o) Cheaper professional and other support costs	
	(p) Less choice in the quality of the support

For the individual staff the diagram could look like this.

STAFF MOVE FORCE-FIELD ANALYSIS

DRIVING FORCES	RESTRAINING FORCES
(a) Better quality of life	
	(b) Perceived loss of facilities (theatres etc.)
	(c) Perceived cultural differences
(d) Better transport/less commuting	
	(e) Scotland has more open spaces – takes longer to get anywhere
(f) Cheaper housing	
	(g) Difficulty of moving back to higher cost areas
(h) Better schooling	
	(i) Less cosmopolitan mix
	(j) Children having to change schools
(k) Better office working conditions	
	(l) Moving from friends and family
	(m) Perceived worse climate
(n) New job opportunities	
	(o) Spouse job change needed
	(p) Further to Europe

In order that the driving and restraining forces can be properly understood, the next stage is to 'weight' each force, effectively giving a value judgement to each item. All members of the brainstorm are asked to apply a value (usually 1 to 10) to each of the identified forces. The average of each person's evaluation of each individual force is then calculated by simple division (i.e. three people give item (a) 6, 4 and 8, so the average weighting is $18 \div 3 = 6$). Note that you will get fractions by this method, so round to the nearest whole number. It is accepted that the technique is subjective and therefore any attempt at too much accuracy is unrealistic. That said, this is as near as can be achieved to 'measuring' a group's perception of driving and restraining forces.

The result can then be displayed on a diagram as follows (where the letters refer to the items on the original force-field chart).

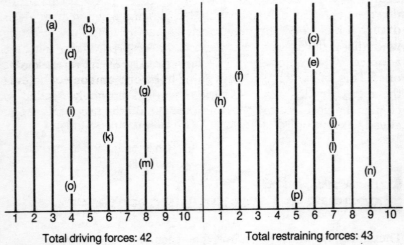

Total driving forces: 42   Total restraining forces: 43

Figure 6.1
Office move force-field analysis (weighting)

There are a number of possible results that can arise. First, there can be a significantly higher number on the 'driving forces' side. This means that generally people agree that change is necessary. It will not meet much resistance overall and a plan for change can begin to be created. However, that is no reason to fail to seek out ways to strengthen the driving forces and weaken the resisting forces. As we will see shortly, some of the resisting forces are often perceived rather than real and a much happier work-force is likely to comply with the change if any unreal fears or doubts are removed.

Secondly, there could be a significantly higher number for restraining forces. This means that the change you are considering may be unwise, at least without further thought and possible modification. To make the change in the face of that perception would be reckless. The company would face massive resistance to its proposals. What may have happened is that the company, in its enthusiasm for a new project, has failed to take into account problems or alternatives which have become obvious to the employees. It may require further brainstorming to modify the proposals to lessen the restraining forces.

Finally, the most common effect in weighting forces is that the figures are balanced, within a sensible range. A few points up or down on either side must be regarded as being equal in an analysis of such subjectivity. This may not mean that there is anything wrong with the proposal for change, but that a programme must be adopted to strengthen the driving forces and weaken the restraining ones. This, of course, is always going to be one outcome whatever the result. In this case, no further work is probably needed to change the proposals at this stage, nor should the proposals yet go ahead without trying to shift the equilibrium.

INCREASING THE DRIVING FORCES

Therefore, we must examine the ways that the company can increase the driving forces and weaken the restraining ones.

Education

Many restraining forces are the result of a combination of lack of knowledge and fear of the unknown. An education programme will often open people's eyes to the truth and automatically reduce restraining forces. In some cases it can turn a restraining force into a strong driving force when misperceptions are cleared up.

Taking the 'staff move' diagram and examples above, the following may be misperceptions that can be rectified by education.

(b) Loss of facilities (theatres etc.)

It may be that the belief that there are many more London theatres is inaccurate; there may be many good theatres in Edinburgh. It may be there are more theatres in Edinburgh per head of population than London and therefore more chance of booking without long waiting periods. Edinburgh also has an arts festival which people visit from all over the world. During this session it might be useful to find out how often people actually go to the theatre, cinema etc. People may see the loss of opportunity as important, when in fact they never use the opportunity anyway. Once this is made visible, people might lessen their resistance. It may also come out during this session that people have other hobbies they actively pursue and that these can be better pursued in Edinburgh.

(m) Perceived worse climate

It may be true that it is colder further north, but there may be advantages. Certainly there are still hot and warm summers, and so on. Perhaps winter is more appreciated in Edinburgh; real snow and not London slush, skiing and tobogganing in the hills and mountains within a short driving distance (which may please the children if not also the adults!). We tend to be creatures of habit; our lifestyle fits the climate we live in and we think that any other climate will upset our lifestyle. An education programme may show how to adapt that lifestyle and increase the quality of life overall.

Finding the missed driving forces to counterbalance the restraining forces

Where there are restraining forces there are often driving forces yet to be discovered. Plan for sessions with your employees to discuss the restraining forces and find the counterbalances. Looking at our examples above we could consider the following.

(c) Perceived cultural differences

Sometimes we forget that the fact an item has been offered as a driving or restraining force may hide the fact that it can be both. In searching for a counterbalance to the question of a restraining force of 'perceived cultural differences' it is easy to overlook the fact that for some people that itself would be a driving force. There are other similar possibilities in the examples below.

(e) Open spaces

Open spaces make people feel good and provide for healthy play for children.

(o) Spouse job change needed

There could be a number of driving forces for this. First, the force-field already indicates that there may be new, even more, job opportunities in the new location. It may also be that the cheaper housing and perhaps other cheaper costs of living in the new location would allow the spouse to take a part-time job and pursue a desired hobby. Alternatively, it may be that the spouse can stop work altogether; this might mean (arguably) that more time could be spent with the children, a counterbalance to the 'problem' of having to change schools.

Training

When considering this aspect we might think about the 'office move' part of the diagram and take point (n) 'Effect on existing customers'. The effect on your customer base may be adverse if you run your company in the same way as you have always done. It may be a problem to serve a customer who was 20 miles away, but is now 450 miles away. The problem may simply be one of recognising that customer's needs and which of those needs you have served in the past. Then staff must be trained to deal with those same needs with no loss of 'comfort factor' as seen from the customer's point of view. That may mean changing your way of operating in order to accom-

modate that customer. For example, it may be that the customer is
used to having one of your sales reps visit once a week. That may not
be possible when the sales force is in Scotland (although if it is an
important customer perhaps you have to make it possible even
then). You could examine what benefit the customer derives from
that visit; if it is just a habitual way of giving a sequence of purchase
orders then you can arrange to fax or telephone. Less frequent visits
may be all that is needed to keep the 'personal' element involved.
You may even discover that the visit has been taking your customer's staff time up, and they are glad to deal with routine matters
more quickly, and leave important matters to fewer visits.

Short-term incentives

Short-term incentives, which could be construed as bribery, must
be used very carefully, and always honestly. They are there to 'prime
the pump', not disguise the truth.

Many companies, for example, pay house moving costs for their
staff if they are required to relocate for their work. Some might
consider 'underwriting' the cost of failure; if the employee does not
like the change in the first six months then the company will pay to
send the person back to where they were, therefore getting over the
problem of moving back to higher cost areas (item (g)).

Even simple, one-off payments of cash to induce moving may be
appropriate. The idea of these payments is to encourage people to
'try out' the change. Often fears are only perceived, and once the
new way of working is in place people learn quickly to like it.
However, there comes a point when bribery must stop. To pay a
person an increased salary just to accept a change, for example,
causes great difficulty when, in five years' time, many local people in
lower wage-rate areas have been employed and either find that
some of their colleagues are being paid more for the same work, or
alternatively the company is paying too much to everyone and ends
up becoming uncompetitive because of its costs.

Thinking ahead of the opposition and discovering their restraining forces to the driving forces

Just because you have a lot of driving forces does not mean that you should not seek out the unknown restraining forces. It is important to ensure that all possibilities have been thought through. It also means you are ahead of the possible opposition that may arise during the years of the change programme. By identifying more restraining forces (by critically examining the driving forces), you will then be able to seek out further counterbalancing restraining forces. At worst, you might suddenly realise that this change programme is doomed to failure – and modify accordingly!

However, in our experience 'doomed' changes are identified quickly even if the people involved fail to take account of the weighting and suffer the consequences of their blinkered approach.

In our 'office move' example we might consider the following.

(a) Cheaper rent and rates

It would be wise to consider whether it is possible to get a rent or rate reduction where you are now. If the balance of the change project is centred around this very significant item and it becomes the most significant reason for the change, the programme will fall apart if you later find you could have got the same advantages where you were before. The balance could instantly shift to a position where the advantage is to stay put.

Alternatively, item (m), 'New markets', may turn out to be a red herring if there is also a saturation of supply in the area or if your company would be 'downgraded' through being new to the area, existing businesses preferring to keep to their traditional, local suppliers.

WHY WEIGHTING WORKS

Just the existence of a driving or restraining force is not enough to measure the depth of feeling about it. Therefore, by weighting we are able to find some measure of strength of feeling. Furthermore, it gets over the inherent problem of the brainstorm: people feel the need to contribute. If they have no strong feelings they will often throw in a suggestion in order to be seen to be taking part. It is important that the analytical stages of the brainstorm take account of those opinions which are strongly held, and those which are just 'contributions for contributions' sake'.

Consider, with your tongue somewhat in your cheek, an extreme situation where the proposed change is to ask someone to leave their house for a week. The restraining forces may be many; fear of burglary, fear of squatters, need to look after the budgie, liking to sit in the garden and so on. If there was only one driving force – that the house was about to be totally destroyed by an approaching meteorite (i.e. to stay was to die!) then that one driving force would be given a weighting that exceeded all the other weightings in the equation.

WHY WEIGHTING DOES NOT WORK

We have demonstrated the shortcomings of force-field weighting in many training and change programme sessions using the proposed change: 'You should dispense with having a car.' The charts emerging from the brainstorm generally look something like this.

OWNING A CAR	
DRIVING FORCES	*RESTRAINING FORCES*
(a) Cars go where public transport does not	
	(b) Capital cost of a car is high
(c) Cars are instantly available for use	
	(d) Traffic jams
(e) Ignoring capital costs, the running costs per mile are cheaper than public transport	
	(f) When a car gets old its running costs get high
	(g) Cars attract vandalism
(h) Prestige	
	(i) Cars need cleaning etc.
(j) Cars are a workhorse (for shopping, DIY etc.)	
(k) Society is structured for use with cars (i.e. supermarkets now out of town, designed for car-drivers)	
(l) Cars are a hobby	
	(m) Government victimises drivers financially; beyond a fair share of 'tax'
	(n) Police operations against drivers are out of proportion to nature of offences

The weighting usually looks something like this.

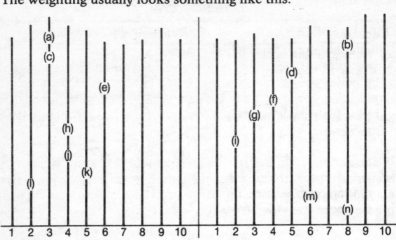

Total driving forces: 27   Total restraining forces: 36

Figure 6.2
Owning a car force-field analysis (weighting)

This sort of pattern is fairly consistent, and is sufficiently weighted in favour of rejecting cars that we believe it ought to be the outcome in a lot of people's minds. That said, we have yet to get anyone in our training sessions to agree that they would give up their car! It is only fair to add here that we do not believe this makes the process invalid; we have tested this sequence in many ways over the years and people *do* respond according to the outcome in most cases. Cars are an exception, for the following reasons.

- (h)   People are afraid to value (on paper) the 'prestige' factor as highly as they truly do in their hearts. Perhaps they are afraid to admit they are emotionally unable to part with their car.
- (k) A desire for independence prevents people from admitting that society is so structured for car-users that they would be severely limited without one. Again, they assign a lower value to this item than they truly feel.
- (m) People will moan about taxation, and use even brainstorming sessions on the subject to 'have their say', but will actually put

up with more unfairness than they claim (a fact which the government's economists no doubt calculate with greater accuracy than individuals!). They assign a higher value to this item than they are prepared to act on.

- (n) Although car drivers apparently do feel unfairly victimised by police they assign a higher value to this item than they are prepared to act on, presumably realising from experience that individually they encounter the police far less frequently than might be feared.

We do not intend to examine this phenomenon further here, but we suggest that the sub-culture surrounding cars is probably more emotional than admitted, and less logical than people would like to present; hence the inconsistent results.

WHEN THE ANALYSIS IS RIGHT, AND ACTED UPON

A good example of a successful analysis correctly acted upon (not necessarily formulated in the way described, but certainly operated in a similar framework of reasoning) was the decision to install automatic ticket barriers at London Underground stations. When it was proposed the idea was met with outcry and opposition: there would be many redundancies; people would not feel safe with the barriers; they needed to meet people and so on. London Underground's governing authority concluded that the weighting of the stated restraining factors was more than outweighed by the driving forces; people could be moved through the barriers faster, speeding up delays in commuting; people may not like impersonal machinery but they would learn to accept it as their dislike was not deep seated and so on. The programme of installation has turned out to be a success. Whether there are other, longer term problems like fewer staff meaning reduced station security is yet to be proven. The aim of the change programme was to introduce and get people used to machinery, and it succeeded.

WHAT HAPPENS WHEN YOU IGNORE THE EQUILIBRIUM

Probably the best example of ignoring the equilibrium was the introduction by the UK government of the community charge (or poll tax) to replace the rates.

Then prime minister Margaret Thatcher presumably believed that the driving forces would outweigh the restraining forces. Whether the government of the day failed to account for all the restraining forces listed below, or simply assigned too small a weighting to them, is unclear, but what is clear (with hindsight) is that the change went ahead when it would have been wiser to have amended the proposal in some way.

Driving forces seem to have been:

- it would be a fairer tax than the rates;
- it would be no less easy to collect;
- it would increase government revenues.

Restraining forces seem to have been:

- even if fairer, there would still be some 'losers' who would be worse off (this was certainly identified);
- there would be bad debts as some people would refuse to pay (identified but perhaps too lightly weighted);
- local government officials opposed to the central government might not enforce the tax enthusiastically (probably identified, but possibly too highly weighted);
- the general population was dissatisfied with Mrs Thatcher and sought a reason for her removal – this became the reason, regardless of the facts about the tax (was this ever considered before the event?);
- there were those in the Conservative party who saw Mrs Thatcher's removal as necessary and who latched on to the 'poll tax' crisis as a reason (does *any* politician recognise when they have become so perceived?).

Whether these factors were considered and under-weighted, or whether they were thought irrelevant, or not thought of at all, we may never know. What remains for us is a clear example of 'getting it wrong', going ahead anyway and then facing the consequences.

▌AFTER THE FORCE-FIELD ANALYSIS
▌IS COMPLETED

The outcome of the force-field analysis, and the brainstorm sessions, is the change project itself, which then has to be devised to take account of the results. Having designed the change project, the next stage is one of implementation. These processes are looked at in the following chapters, but first it would be useful to try out a force-field analysis for yourself.

Faced with having to begin a brainstorm and force-field analysis it is best to have confidence in the process. Actually, we do force-field analysis informally every day of our lives, but it is wise to try out a small, personal one on paper to 'get the feel of it'. See the 'dishwasher problem' below. Alternatively, think about the times you ignored the messages of an informal force-field analysis, for one reason or another, and then spent a good deal of time afterwards regretting it! We have all done that at some time.

Force field analysis – personal test example

The problem of the first-time purchase of a dishwasher for home use.

Possible driving forces

1. Not having to wash up.
2. Not having to dry up.
3. Fewer arguments in the family as to who will wash up.
4. Items washed better.
5. Kinder to hands.

Possible restraining forces

1. The capital cost of buying a dishwasher.
2. The increased use of electricity and water.
3. Installation of dishwasher causing disruption to the design of the kitchen.
4. Arguments as to who is going to load and unload the dishwasher.
5. Insurance and maintenance costs.

With regard to weighting, not having to wash up may have a higher weighting than, say, kindness to hands (which could be solved by wearing rubber gloves). The cost of the dishwasher may have to be balanced against forgoing a holiday or a new video. The cost of increased use of electricity and water has to be balanced against the saving in water heating costs.

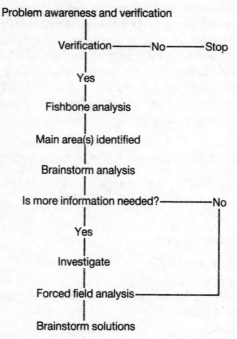

Figure 6.3
Problem-solving process

WHERE FORCE-FIELD ANALYSIS FITS INTO PROBLEM SOLVING

Force-field analysis is one of the techniques and tools of problem solving that change managers will want to use in work groups. It links problem identification with brainstorming for solutions.

The flowchart in Figure 6.3 demonstrates how to establish if a problem exists. It then sets out the various steps in the problem-solving process, showing where force-field analysis fits into the approach.

First, we verify that there is a problem (if there is not then there is no need to go any further!). Having verified that there is a problem the first analysis of that problem can be done by fishbone analysis which identifies the main areas of the subject.

Results of this are then brainstormed (i.e. openly and radically debated and discussed), and the possible need for more information identified.

After all the information is finally collated the force-field analysis can be undertaken.

7 | THE EFFECT OF CHANGE UPON THE INDIVIDUAL

FEARS ABOUT CHANGE

Corporate change programmes can have a disturbing effect on the individuals affected by their consequences. We have considerable experience of change projects where we have acted as consultants and change-project team leaders. This experience shows clearly that in most organisations change is – at least initially – perceived as a threat (or potential threat) to an individual's status, habits, beliefs and behaviour.

Status

We should never underestimate the disappointment that people in organisations are caused when their status at work is changed. Such changes may be minor in reality – perhaps just a change of job titles or a reduction in the numbers of people working in their teams. Another significant status symbl is budget allocation; the amount of budget under an individual's signature is deemed to be a company's estimate of a person's value and any alterations must be handled carefully.

Status is important to the individual. It is part of their personal development within the organisation in so far that they have striven to reach the status they presently have. Status is equivalent to recognition. Often, any disturbance in status is seen as a threat to, or reduction in, the recognition given to them by the organisation.

Habits and personal beliefs

People are creatures of habit and feel safe in routine. Many seek out repetitive work with predesignated breaks for tea, lunch, meetings and so on. Change often disturbs that comfortable pattern of habits of working. People are disturbed and disrupted until new habits and patterns are given chances to develop.

People believe in themselves. Their confidence is built up from an ability to deal with situations as they know them to be. Change threatens to create new situations that people are unfamiliar with and may cause them to lose faith in themselves, i.e. in their ability to cope with their new environment. Also, people believe in their kit, i.e. the machinery and working systems they are used to. Change often includes new kit, and threatens to make obsolete those who cannot transfer from the old systems to the new.

People also believe in their staff and colleagues. They learn to rely on them to get the job done well. Change processes introduce new people who themselves introduce further new kit, new methods, new systems and new ways of working. People are threatened by these changes because they fear that they will eventually make them obsolete. The new people may deal more efficiently with the new systems they themselves have introduced.

Behaviour

We have all built up a repertoire of behaviours in both our social lives and our jobs. Change means that we may have to discard some of these behaviours and learn new ones. Eventually we have to show our new behaviour to our colleagues, team members, customers and so on.

Generally, this is unsettling; it takes time through practice to become as comfortable with the new behaviours as we were with the old. The individual is therefore involved in a process by which he or she is having to unlearn one process and learn a new way of working.

For the above reasons, resistance to change is natural. The first thing that change managers have to understand is that it is not irrational to fear the consequences of change; indeed it would be irrational not to have doubts. Resistance is diminished by removing the doubts and replacing the unknown with certainties.

The job of the change manager is first to encourage open debate about the change through encouraging those affected by it to express their doubts and misgivings. They must not allow people to escape into closed thinking by indifference, lack of effort and subsequent low morale. Change managers must work to avoid suspicion of management motives for introducing the change, and social upset caused by working with different people in new ways.

WHAT WE KNOW ABOUT CHANGE

Our experience with change programmes has given us insights into the way change works, and the effects it has.

Change is a learning process

Change is a training experience for individuals. Properly devised, it should be part of a corporate training programme that develops both the individual and the company. For the company, such development is concerned with corporate teambuilding.

There is a greater concentration at the present time on tasks being dealt with by teams in order to create continuity. The move to team structures in organisations is one of the widest changes we are seeing. Teambuilding is a subject covered in our book *Managing Your Team* (Piatkus).

People learn at different rates, and a planned programme of change must be flexible enough to allow for that. It is not possible to put a whole group of people into a training room and expect them all to assimilate and accept the change programme in the same way, or over the same period of time.

Furthermore, different people learn in quite different ways. There are some who learn best by rote (remember standing in class reciting the two-times table, the three-times table and so on?), while many others learn best by experience. Generally, though not exclusively, the most adaptable minds are those that have learned to learn by experience. In training, experience can be delivered to delegates through simulations, role-play, brainstorming, problem-analysis, video presentations and so on. For this learning process to develop fully, training must include on-site, actual experience. (See Chapter 10 for more on ways of training for change.)

Unfortunately for many of us, school training, until a few years ago, was mostly done by rote. This failed totally in preparing people to spend the rest of their lives learning by experience. The modern teaching methods in schools allow for people to 'learn how to learn', so we are now seeing a more flexible work-force and management emerging. Such flexibility will make the future introduction of change programmes easier.

Change is a response

Change occurs after an event, rather than in advance of the need for it. Very few companies are proactive to change, having been taught that 'if it ain't broke, don't fix it'. This may be true in some situations, but companies must develop a proactive stance towards change, despite considerable inertia in companies in which it is said that 'necessity is the mother of invention'. Companies have not learned to anticipate necessities; therefore the acceptance of change is an invention that is rarely planned for ahead of need.

Change is discontinuous

It would be nice if change were a smooth, flowing process. However, it is rarely so. In most companies change is a stop–start process, with long periods of inactivity, which can be caused by management losing faith in the change programme or by the introduction of a newer idea.

In one of the companies where we consulted we found that a change programme that had been installed two years prior to our work was to be resurrected. The work-force thought 'it had gone away, and all the fuss had died down', whereas management were unaware that anyone believed that the programme was being pursued anything less than enthusiastically!

Change is the sum of small changes

There are no great and dramatic changes in organisations, except perhaps corporate collapses (which cannot count since they are not – usually – part of a plan). What change really means in organisations is a collection of small changes. This might mean departmental changes or redesigns, divisional changes or a process of devolving power to small local offices (or perhaps the reverse, a concentration of devolved power back to the central HQ). There may be changes in the factory to certain procedures, perhaps health and safety driven. Properly controlled and planned, these changes cascade down into a waterfall of major change. By the end of the process the fact of change is apparent, but along the way it is less obvious.

Change is a long-term activity

Any significant, planned change programme is a plan for years ahead, not just weeks or months. Because companies have developed their ways of operating over years, so it will take years for major change to arise. It is a balanced equation; changing a small area of work takes small effort, while changing a major aspect of work takes either major effort or a very long time. Change programmes are designed to encourage major effort and save the time, since taking a long time would let the competition get ahead.

Change needs high levels of motivation

Motivation is covered in detail in Chapter 8. However, a question that we might ask at this stage is why we put so much effort into change projects dealing with people who we have made unsuccessful and demotivated. People must be motivated, and allowed to enjoy success at work, before we can ask them to accept change programmes.

It might seem that someone unhappy at work would welcome change; in fact this is rarely the case. Most people who are unhappy at work become concerned that change is a threat to them personally. In this chapter we look at how to handle that situation.

We have assisted in several change projects and found considerable resistance from the staff. On further examination we discovered that there were strong demotivating factors at work that we had not been made aware of. In one particular case we were taking the work-force through a change programme when we discovered – 'by accident' through talking to the delegates – that a pay freeze had been instigated and a vague threat of redundancy made. Whether the work-force believed this was part of the change project or not was unclear; certainly they were in no mood to co-operate with the company.

Change needs reinforcement

One of the effects of change programmes is that organisation charts need to be redrawn in order to explain and accommodate the changes. Because change is a constant process (or at least should be!), there will have to be many new organisation charts. Furthermore, because change involves a 'ripple effect' (one change leading to more changes), organisation charts in affected departments may need to be revised periodically. This can give the impression that the company do not know what they are doing; that they are 'trying to get it right'. To avoid that allegation, and the doubt that it causes in the minds of those affected by change, it is important to explain at the outset that it will happen. Where possible, give some details of the long-term plan and how changes are likely to be phased in.

The change machine may need oiling

Although we always stress the fact that change is only facilitated through long-term planning and a programme of enlightenment (bringing the work-force to a degree of understanding), we realise that sometimes short-term measures have to be taken. Regard these measures as priming the change-pump. Such managerial interventions may include paying bonuses for accepting changed working conditions, offering overtime, company perks and so on. These interventions are bribes, we might as well honestly admit! In the long term they would be demotivating (see Chapter 8), but in the short term they may encourage a resistant work-force or managerial level to 'have a go'. Hopefully, once hooked into the process, the longer term enlightenment can then begin.

THE STAGES OF CHANGE

In any change situation the effect of change upon the individual can be monitored. Most people have similar reactions to the various stages of change. What follows is a summary of the various stages that people go through in any change situation.

Stage 1   The honeymoon period

We must assume, at this point, that the change process has been sold effectively to the staff by management (see Chapter 8 on how to do this). They will have explained the vision of the new culture and carefully described how and why the change must happen. They will have spelt out the benefits and rewards of accepting the change to both the individual and the organisation. Assuming that they have been succesful, the first stage of change can be described as 'the honeymoon period'.

Although the staff do not yet know much about what the change involves, for example, what effort is needed and the possible outcomes that are likely, they are often excited at this stage. People usually feel very positive about the outcomes. This stage can be short, or can last a long period of time, depending on how well people are trained and how quickly they are able to discover the facts about the change.

The truth is that the euphoria of this period is caused by a combination of ignorance of what is happening, and reassurance from (trusted) senior management that it will be beneficial. This stage could be summed up by the warcry, 'Yeah! That sounds great – let's go for it!'

It is sensible to consider, by way of analogy and example, a change process that we all undergo at some time in our lives – moving house. The honeymoon period is the time when the move represents more and bigger rooms, a bigger garden, a neighbourhood that we perceive as better and so on. We have not yet considered the stress of moving, the difficulties of redecoration, the effect on the children of changing schools, the possibility of unpleasant neighbours.

All changes in our personal and business lives have a honeymoon period – getting married, buying a new car, starting an affair, planning a holiday and so on. The excitement and euphoria of all such endeavours are based on lack of knowledge and a belief that 'all will be well'.

Stage 2   The discomfort period

The honeymoon period usually gives way to a state of discomfort as initial optimism about the change process gives way to self-doubt and doubts about the organisation. What happens in this discomfort period is that people begin to question the need for change on the (expected and normal) basis that they have been working in a certain way for years and the change implies that they have been doing it wrong (because they are being asked to do the same thing in a different way). Defensive questions are raised, such as 'Why should we change when we make a profit etc.?'

In our house-moving analogy, real fears that might, for example, be based on questions like 'Can we afford the new higher mortgage?' are translated into such phrases as 'Well, do we really need to move, after all this house has done us proud for five years?', and so on.

Stage 3   The discovery period

After people have worked through the honeymoon period and the period of doubts and questioning, the next natural stage of change is 'the discovery period'.

At this stage, people begin to learn more about what change entails and what they will have to do to make it happen. They start observing the reactions of other people to the change process. Further doubts arise and it becomes increasingly difficult to maintain the previous, positive attitude. This third stage is usually reached fairly quickly. Unfortunately, many people get stuck in this stage and the company is often faced with individuals' cynicism. People often *want* to stay in this stage because it's perceived as 'anti-establishment'; by resistance they can become heroes for fifteen minutes (Andy Warhol style). The signs that people are in this stage are indifference, lack of action and paying lip-service (and lip-service *only*) to the change process.

The discovery period is accompanied by the denial process that goes with it. We have been working very closely in change projects for major UK corporations and we have observed that the initial enthusiasms, i.e. the honeymoon period, quickly gave way to denial that the change was in fact new, or any real change at all. The most popular comment seems to be something like: 'This is nothing new to me. I have been a quality manager for the past twenty years and they just didn't call it that in my day', and so on.

In our spread of clients, ranging from hospitals in the USA, oil exploration companies, petrochemical companies, retail organisations, manufacturing industries, financial institutions, and a Euro-theme park and leisure companies we have seen that this effect is across the board, which has convinced us that it is a natural part of the change process.

This denial process is natural, but having expressed their resistance people then begin to 'buy into' – and side with – the change procedures. It is important that change managers are aware of this stage. If everybody talks themselves into convincing everybody else that 'We were all doing that anyway', it dilutes the total effect of change and diminishes the goals that we need to achieve.

Stage 4   The experimental period

The next, experimental stage of change reveals a positive attitude and willingness to exert effort, where people begin to do things in the new way, and watch what effect it is having upon the systems and others. This stage takes time. The experimenters need support as mistakes are bound to happen; the learning curves are only just being established.

This is often the most exciting part of the change process, with new ideas, new methods and new technologies being used for the known corporate goals. What at first seemed difficult slowly starts to become possible and, like a jigsaw puzzle finally coming together, the big picture starts to appear. At this point the change managers must coach, encourage, push and – most of all – get involved with their teams and their staff. This transition from the discovery period to the experimental period is a very emotional time for the people undergoing the changes. What is happening here is that the ideas and new working methods, i.e. the new ways of doing things, are now being transferred from the abstract to the concrete. The talking is over, the script is written, the rehearsals are done; it is now time to go on stage in front of your first real audience and act the part. The change manager must give strong support and allow emotions to be brought into the open. Mostly, he or she will accomplish this through brainstorming sessions examining the issues and the problems as they affect individuals and teams.

To continue our analogy, we are now living in our new house; we are getting used to the neighbours and the neighbourhood, we are enjoying the extra space and so on.

Stage 5   The consolidation period

The final stage of change is consolidation. Here, the new change process is fitted into the structure and culture of the organisation. Here we can observe in individuals a sense of satisfaction and accomplishment; they have managed to overcome their own obstacles and objections to the change process. They have confronted and dealt with the obstacles and objections of others.

The problem with this stage is that people often get bored with it as the exciting work is now done. How many people move house, spend five years redecorating and rebuilding, construct extensions, landscape the garden and then sit back and almost immediately plan to move again? It is common enough – the pursuit of the ideal house is more fun than actually finding it.

The final push from the experimental stage to the consolidation stage needs careful planning and monitoring. Often, as we begin to learn more about the new ways of doing things, we need to go back to the experimental stages again and again. Indeed, any continued improvement process demands that we constantly monitor and modify our new working methods. Again, the change manager must give strong support to the experimenters as they go back and forward between experiment and consolidation.

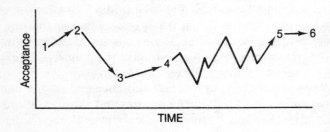

1	= Identification that change is needed
1–2	= The honeymoon period
2–3	= The period of discomfort
3–4	= The discovery period
4–5	= The experimental period
5–6	= The consolidation period
6	= Successful installation

Figure 7.1
The cycle of change

▌INDIVIDUALS AND STRESS

An important part of the job of those implementing change is to relieve stress. This is a common response to change, and the change managers must identify and assist those who suffer stress because of their fears of the changes under way.

What is stress?

Stress is often defined as being what happens when someone is pushed beyond their capabilities. If stress is allowed to build up, then even after the stress-causing factors are removed there is often not a full return to the previous, unstressed state. It is analogous to one person's description of living through an earthquake; even after it was over they felt for years that they could never trust the earth not to move again.

In the context of change much stress is the result of a person fearing they will be pushed beyond their limit, rather than being caused by a tangible reality. If those handling the change programme can identify sources of fear, and those people likely to be concerned, then just by describing the effects of the change, and allowing those with fears to voice them, much potential stress can be avoided.

What underlies stress?

Stress is most obvious when work ceases to become a challenge and a source of stimulation, and becomes threatening instead. The detailed causes of stress in a change situation are manifold. The following list is not exhaustive, but represents the most common factors. Some of these factors are conflicting and will only arise in certain change situations, so not all are therefore likely to arise:

- a fear of increased, and unwelcome, responsibility;
- a fear of being too closely supervised and not allowed to get on with the job;
- a fear of unreasonable productivity demands;
- a fear that new working procedures will give rise to conflicting or unclear priorities;
- a general dislike of disruption caused by change, much of which is possibly imagined;
- a fear that an existing job will become of less value;
- a fear that new procedures and structure will block promotion, make expectations unlikely, and even lead to redundancy;
- 'challenge overload', where there is never a respite – when one problem is conquered the next is already lurking on the horizon.

The irrational element of any of the above can be removed by talking through the fears and explaining the true situation. Even if some of the fears above are likely to be justified, and will arise, in most cases a better knowledge of the details of the change are less stressful than fear of the unknown.

In addition, the change agents can negotiate with individuals to find compromises that may alleviate stress, amending proposed routines, job-changes and so on, to meet their needs.

How can you identify stress?

People under stress may exhibit the following behaviour:

* unusual tiredness;
* increased absenteeism;
* increased nervousness;
* the onset of illnesses like headaches and unusual pains, also breathlessness, exceptional weight-change, indigestion and stomach-related problems;
* irrational anxiety, in other words more anxiety being focused on a task than it really deserves;
* a tendency to blame others, perhaps more than usual;
* inability to prioritise work rationally;
* inability to make firm decisions, or displaying poor judgement;
* displaying an irrational bad temper;
* claiming they are too busy to take a holiday;
* failing to finish work well within their capabilities, and a reluctance to take on tasks (which they perceive as being beyond their capabilities);
* working late or taking work home in the evenings;
* arriving late for meetings, or arriving unprepared;
* not caring about their appearance as much as they used to;
* alcoholism or drug abuse;
* not seeming to have fun any more.

People under stress will exhibit some obvious and sometimes dramatic changes in behaviour. Once alerted, the aware manager will identify many of the above traits to some degree. Not all traits will appear in all people, though these are the commonest found.

When you have identified someone who may be under stress, remember that in the context of a change programme the first way to avoid stress is to talk to the person and make visible their fears.

Some of the stress may indeed by justified. In designing the programme for change you may have overlooked practical factors that others have considered. Be ready to address these issues and amend your plan if necessary. Such issues may be:

- new, and ill-thought out, administrative policies;
- changed health and safety routines;
- introduction of inappropriate staff or contractors;
- inadequate training for new procedures;
- changed physical working conditions.

We have set out above the common symptoms of stress in the work-place. Unfortunately some companies have routines set up to deal with the symptoms, but they fail to consider the underlying causes – or deny that they are a company problem. Companies which are concerned to counter stress – in change programmes or any other circumstances – should consider the benefits to the work-force of actively promoting good physical and mental health.

- Encourage exercise and diet in a practical way. For example, one company we know paid for its staff to go on daily aerobic workouts of half an hour, and laid on fresh fruit and vegetables at lunch time. They were certain that they got increased efficiency from their staff throughout the working day. Sir Ralph Halpern, former chief executive of Burtons, had a gymnasium built in the company's West End head office as an alternative to the executive lunch. One of us attended meetings on a particular project with that company and many senior retailers of the group would walk into the meeting with a Mars bar after their hour's work-out!
- Larger companies may be able to provide educational training in matters relating to physical and mental health.
- Provide training which allows people to plan their time and priorities.
- Companies can 'desensitise' people to stress through simulating the new environment in training, by running workshops for involved staff.

The experience of those in the American Space Programme shows just how effective such simulations can be when taken to extremes. NASA officials were concerned about the well-being and perform-ance of early astronauts on the Mercury programme. This was the first American-manned space-flight programme, and astronauts would be flying alone in a tiny, cramped capsule, reaching into an environment totally alien to humans. To desensitise them each astronaut was put in a simulator that created the image of flying around the Earth, in orbit. The astronauts were put through these simulations so frequently and persistently that one participant – Alan Shepard – found that reality did not feel real. Where reality differed from the simulations it felt as if reality was at fault!

Women and stress

There are specific causes of stress relating to women in the working environment. Whereas the above factors apply to both sexes, women are presently subject to additional factors.

- Conflict with home responsibilities. Whereas the future may well hold a more equal division of home responsibilities, at the present time the majority of households expect the woman in a family group to deal with 'running the home'. A change that offers promotion might be welcomed by a man, but may cause stress in a woman if she feels that it will create conflict with her other responsibilities, or conflict with her partner. Discussion of the implications of such promotion will help to alleviate the stress. Help and advice for dealing with male stereotypical images may be offered by more progressive companies.
- Women may feel that new procedures will expose them to dis-crimination.
- Women may be under more pressure to succeed than men. They may feel that they have more to prove, or are 'standard-bearers' for women in general. Such perceived responsibility can cause considerable stress.
- Women who are being used as 'token' or 'experimental' women in a new procedure or environment may feel resentful, and may find the attitude condescending.

- In a predominantly male environment women have no peer group for support.
- Women leaders have fewer role models. While this can be an advantage in that their own talents can come to the fore, it can cause stress because of uncertainty.
- Women who complain may be perceived as 'feminist' when the same complaint from a man would be acceptable.
- Attributes that are thought laudable in men (power, assertiveness, hunger for success) are sometimes regarded as undesirable in women, while at the same time they have to compete with men on just those terms for promotion and opportunity.
- Women, not exclusively, but more than men, suffer sexual harassment.
- Women are subject to 'politically correct' pressure groups who demand they act in a certain way in order to promote the group's political aims with which the women themselves may not sympathise. This conflict can cause considerable stress.

Specific solutions arise from dealing with specific issues intelligently. However, as a general solution, part of the change process has to be the recognition of women as equal candidates for all positions in a company. At the present time that will mean *positive* discrimination to enable women to choose between, or accommodate both, career and personal responsibilities.

As a simple example, there are still far too few crèches in companies, even with government tax concessions as encouragement. The longer term attitude changes that might be required in both men and women to facilitate longer term changes are outside the scope of this book.

PERSONAL STRESS MANAGEMENT

Complete this checklist. It will assess your ability to cope with the potential stresses of working life, and your lifestyle.

To what degree, on a scale of 1 to 6, do the following statements apply to you? Be truthful – you're only fooling yourself otherwise!

1 = Very rarely true
6 = Usually true

		Very rarely true				Usually true	
1.	I do not take on more tasks than I can deal with	1	2	3	4	5	6
2.	I plan my lifestyle to be healthy	1	2	3	4	5	6
3.	I don't let things get me down	1	2	3	4	5	6
4.	My personal life is in control	1	2	3	4	5	6
5.	I know how to 'switch off' and relax	1	2	3	4	5	6
6a.	I organise my work into urgent and non-urgent tasks	1	2	3	4	5	6
6b.	I organise my work into important and non-important tasks	1	2	3	4	5	6
7.	I plan for time off work (and take it)	1	2	3	4	5	6
8.	I get enough sleep	1	2	3	4	5	6
9.	I am strong enough to say *no* if someone asks me to do something	1	2	3	4	5	6
10.	I have an active and fulfilling life outside work	1	2	3	4	5	6
11.	I recover from bad moods and 'bad days' quickly	1	2	3	4	5	6
12.	I expect to enjoy life at work and home – and I do!	1	2	3	4	5	6

Obviously the higher the score the more likely you are to be coping with stress.

A score of 1 to 26 indicates that you are severely prone to suffering stress. This may, at the extreme, indicate that you are in the wrong job. More likely it reflects an unhealthy attitude towards your job. Take the time to consider what goals you want to achieve in life, and then ask yourself if your present job is likely to allow you to achieve those goals. Most stress is caused not by what we do, but by the things we leave undone – you may be failing to finish tasks and consequently suffering from feeling low achievement levels.

Score 27–52   You are probably coping well with your job and feeling comfortable in your present position. The average score indicates that there are times when you are stressed, or it might be that certain areas of your work are causing stress. Take the time to analyse the specific situations that cause you stress and consider whether you dealt with them well. It may be that some training (i.e. assertiveness, presentation skills etc.) is all that is needed to overcome certain areas of your work-day problems.

Score 53–78   You are not one for suffering stress. While that must be cause for celebration, ask yourself if you are stretching yourself enough, or if you are resting on your laurels for a little too long! The absence of stress is not necessarily a good thing – a little stress can be motivational. You're not bored are you?

8

MOTIVATING FOR CHANGE

▌UNDERSTANDING MOTIVATION

In devising a change programme the change agents must understand that change itself is *not* a motivation. It may be that people look forward to changes – not all changes are resisted. However, the normal factors which motivate people still need to be in place, and there may be a need for new, perhaps temporary, factors to encourage people to accept the changes. In order to devise such motivations management must understand how and why individuals are motivated.

Coercion and fear

Outdated methods of motivation include coercion and fear. Smaller organisations still use such methods. Sadly, small-minded managers in large companies have not yet learned to put such methods behind them either.

Fear can be used to manipulate people within a spectrum from rumour to overt aggression. In business, managers create fear by using threats of redundancy, relocation, change of job status and so

on. Unfortunately, if change programmes are not well communicated people can also fear just these threats when they are not
intended. Conversely, some change programmes involve just these
outcomes, when the only proper attitude on the part of the change
managers is to communicate them quickly and fairly. It is
uncertainty that causes stress; even bad news is usually less stressful
if there are no doubts.

While people feel that their jobs are threatened, even if they are
not, they will be unsettled, and they will work at only the minimum
level required to remain in the organisation.

More subtle threats are often used. For example, when the CEO
of the company asks you to do something it carries the implication
of threat; more so than when your line manager gives the same
order. In practical terms the CEO may have less opportunity to use
their influence against you, but their 'presence' is strong.

Motivation is often achieved by manoeuvring individuals into
circumstances where they believe that their best course of action is
to comply with your demands, threats and so on. Those being
manipulated do not have the opportunity to achieve goals of their
own. Their best perceived outcome is to emerge from the circumstances without losing – they don't expect to win. One of the most
common forms of such manipulation is where companies offer
promotion or relocation, while at the same time hinting that refusal
would mean no other such offers or promotions.

Money as a motivator

Positive motivation techniques encourage people to act in the way
you want them to because they can achieve goals of their own.
Money can be such a motivator – but only to a point. If people are
paid more they will perform better over the very short term. To
expect such motivation to last for a longer term is not only naïve, but
– to the recipient of such bribes – it can be actually insulting.

If a person is not paid what they believe themselves to be worth
then they will not feel motivated. They will work below their best,
and they will be unresponsive to change programmes, seeing them
as 'always working for the bosses, but never for me'. There comes a
point, however, when individuals recognise that they are being paid

a reasonable wage. If people think they are being overpaid, or if they feel they are being bribed, they become resentful and angry. This is compounded if their personal circumstances do not easily let them give up their job. Theirs is a catch-22 situation, for which they will blame their company.

Motivation has then ceased; they have other goals that need to be met. The most important of these goals is usually the appreciation of a person's work. If a person does not feel that their work is of value, or making a significant contribution to the business, they will not be motivated.

In conclusion then, money used as a reward becomes a norm and increased supplies of money are then required to achieve the same level of activity or commitment, like a drug addict craving more and more to satisfy his or her need. Eventually the need cannot be met; motivation ceases.

Theory X and Theory Y

People have different individual needs. They arise from past experiences and beliefs of how those experiences will affect the environment they are working in. Motivation must reflect those experiences and beliefs.

Organisations seeking to instigate change programmes must demonstrate changed behaviour. They must act in a different way if they seek to get others to act in a different way.

In *The Human Side of Enterprise*, Douglas McGregor divided people into two groups with a different approach to motivation; this he summed up as Theory X and Theory Y. Theory X represents traditional methods of controlling people, while Theory Y is the more enlightened and empowering approach. Theory X suggests that by nature the typical employee is lazy, doesn't like work, is unambitious, will avoid responsibility, is passive, and is moved by punishment and reward. Such a person, the theory argues, needs rigid supervision because he or she has no self-discipline.

Theory Y is the opposite. It suggests that the average employee enjoys work and finds it satisfying or punishing, depending on circumstances. Such people are thought to be willing and able to take responsibility.

On this basis the motivating forces are already inherent in the work-force. Problems arise when a Theory Y-oriented management has to manage a change programme through Theory X systems. From our experience, what has now developed is Theory Y-oriented senior management and staff who want to be treated in a Theory Y manner, but who are being led and managed by Theory X middle management.

We believe that the reason why middle management adopt Theory X is because they are having to operate the organisation along codes of practice and work systems developed and enhanced in an environment based on Theory X. There is no doubt that Theory Y is attractive. However, Theory Y cannot become the norm unless we are prepared to introduce more Theory Y systems and procedures into our organisations.

Hierarchy of needs

For change managers seeking to motivate individuals towards accepting changes the 'hierarchy of needs' developed by psychologist Abraham Maslow is vitally important. As its name implies Maslow's proposal was that needs could be ranked in a hierarchy; before dealing with 'higher' level needs those lower down the scale had to be satisfied:

The hierarchy is displayed in Figure 8.1.

The lowest level of needs are the **basic needs**: food, drink, shelter and rest, for example. Clearly these needs will be paramount in an individual's mind if they are not satisfied, and no other needs will have significance until they are. Imagine trying to help victims of Third World famine by addressing their social and ego needs when they desperately need food, for example. Comedian Billy Connolly tells the story of goodwill being delivered to the deprived part of Glasgow he once lived in; when the children wanted food and shoes, the authorities built them a library. (His punch-line was that they strapped the books to their feet!)

In the developed areas of the globe the majority of people find these needs satisfied through their salaries. However, we live in a fragile world; the recession of the late 1980s and early 1990s hit – more than ever before – the 'small' businessperson who tradi-

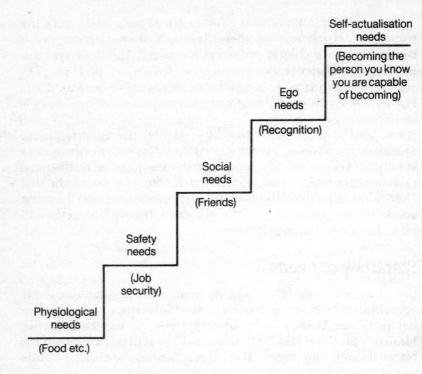

Figure 8.1
Maslow's hierarchy of needs

tionally put up his or her home as security for bank borrowings. The difficult trading conditions resulted in many people losing their homes, and their resultant anger was a recognition that people quickly revert down the scale of needs to the most basic when they are threatened. Most luxury items were given up as people concentrated on food, warmth and paying the mortgage (if they still had one). For change managers it is important to recognise that any change which threatens these basic needs will be resisted most strongly. Perhaps more importantly, wrong information or poor communication about the change programme that implies a threat to these basic needs will be resisted and even rejected through fear before the truth is known.

The second set of needs to be satisfied are **safety needs**. In our society protection against deprivation is a factor of job security. If there are badly communicated threats of redundancy, what often happens is that the best people will seek to protect themselves by searching for alternative work. It may be that these people would not have been targets for redundancy anyway, but because of their skills they may be the most mobile and able to react to their fears. If there are to be redundancies the proper course of action is to announce them as soon as possible, and as specifically as possible. It helps to reassure those who are not being made redundant that their jobs are safe.

With these basic needs catered for people then aspire to **social needs**; the need to work in teams, to form friendships at work. Since most modern companies operate teams of varying size and duration, for most tasks this need is actively catered for. It is worth considering an example where the opposite was tried, and failed. One large computer services company had a team of computer programmers all working in one building. Each member of the staff had his or her own work-station containing their computer and whatever other back-up they needed. The company reasoned that there was no requirement for these individuals to work together and decided that each member of the staff could work from home. They paid for, and organised, the move of each individual's work-station to their home, and rewarded the staff with compensation for their office-at-home. There would be no difference in the work, they thought, since the work took place in the computer with the programmers working as individuals. As a spin-off they saved a lot of money in not having to lease the offices they had been using.

The result was a disaster: quality of work dropped; morale dropped. Two problems were identified: first there was no longer any informal brainstorming of ideas, so creativity was affected. Secondly, the team mentality died; the time spent 'by the coffee machine', chatting in the corridors, talking to each other in front of the washbasins was suddenly recognised as important. This was the time when people sparked each other off. It was where the corporate mentality had been built that was lost when the people were physically kept away from each other. Companies like IBM and BT are reported to have been experimenting with solutions to this kind of problem.

People at work need people. Even the most isolationist of people (with the odd exception) need someone to communicate with. The change programme that threatens that will not work. Fortunately, most large companies have realised this point already. Smaller companies are begining to catch up with this; there is great emphasis in recruitment on such phrases as 'we're a family company'.

The trend towards 'working from home' is growing, though, in fact, many people find their home the wrong environment for work. Many senior executives displaced by large companies have set themselves up as independent management consultants and subsequently one of the more interesting trends has been for them to form loose associations with other independent consultants. They have done this by setting up small office facilities where they can share information-technology systems etc. More importantly they can receive the social interaction missing when 'working from home'. Evidence for these associations can be seen in joint advertising, and the rise of 'serviced', group, offices. This trend is also becoming apparent with secretaries working from home, encouraged by the availability of low-cost but comfortable offices on short-term leases.

There are obvious costs to be saved by sharing less frequently used equipment such as fax machines, photocopiers etc. People we have spoken to are quite open in the view that the cross-fertilisation of work is of less importance than the ability to meet, socialise and also share problems – and therefore problem solving.

In one particular instance a group of independent chartered accountants formed a weekly luncheon club (called the 'Steak and Kidney Pudding Club') in order to alleviate the isolation of working on their own.

Larger companies, having dealt with the above, are beginning to look at the **higher level (ego) needs**: recognition by the organisation, self-esteem needs, self-confidence and seeking knowledge. Few companies have yet achieved this, or even addressed the question properly. Recognition is still defined all too often as a pat on the back and a hearty 'Well done'. There is nothing wrong with either, but recognition of a person's worth should go much deeper than that. It is a matter of placing trust in a person, of really listening to them (with open ears, not open mouths!) and of allowing them to take ownership of their work.

Companies are trying to address these points, but it often amounts to only lip-service as yet. Self-confidence comes from being able to try, and not be punished for failure. Companies that encourage people to take risks help themselves and their staff to develop their best potential. From failure we learn how to succeed; from success we rarely learn anything other than how to fear failure.

The change programmes of the future must address this level of needs; companies that fail to do so will lose their best staff to those companies that do.

The last stage of the hierarchy was the level of **self-actualisation needs**. This is the need we all have to become the person we believe we have the potential to become.

Far from being encouraged in most companies, the majority of middle management actively discourage satisfying this need. The most cynical view of this would be that, having been brought up in a Theory X environment, most managers fear they would be surpassed by their own staff if they 'became the people they had the potential to become'. The managers themselves simply have little option for such development. As we stated earlier, many of them have followed a limited path to their present position, based on copying the mistakes of managements before them. This brings us back to the point that change programmes must address all levels of the organisation, and be ruthless in parts.

Maslow's hierarchy allows the change programme to be devised, taking into account the stages people have to go through before they can give their full potential to the organisation. It also highlights those areas that will prevent people giving their best.

OUTSOURCING AND SUBCONTRACTING

One of the most fundamental changes that has been happening in recent years in large companies is outsourcing and subcontracting.

This seems to threaten people's need for job security and can de-motivate. Job security – at least in the conventional sense – is now much less common in companies. The 'job for life' is a thing of the past. Many firms, particularly those who are affected by cyclical trading, have replaced full-time employees with contractors. Such contractors are often ex-employees. Contractors are deemed to have less job security as they can be 'used' when needed and not used when there is no work. The company saves money by not having to pay for 'idle time', but the contractor is only paid when needed. This often means that a subcontractor cannot depend on his or her income (true of any self-employed person, of course).

However, in most cases (unless under a contract that prevents it), subcontractors can work for several 'employers'. By doing so they have a better chance of earning their full pay. The additional advantage is that all their eggs are not in one basket; as recessions show, jobs are not 'secure' and it only takes one employer to sack you. For the self-employed subcontractor with ten or twenty clients, one client 'sacking' him or her is not so crucial. So we may be seeing a new form of job security in this move that is, in any case, taking place in a mobile work-force.

One effect of the subcontracting route is that such individuals consequently form fewer friendships and other social affiliations at work. Social needs are becoming more neglected; social clubs, societies and sports teams are closing down. There has been, however, an increase in people's confidence and independence as they realise that training in transferrable skills, mobility and adaptability are more immediately important than needs of recognition and self-esteem. And that training is now being catered for in many companies.

▌MOTIVATION EFFECTS OF CHANGE ▌ON TEAMS

Since most work in companies is performed in a team environment change managers must consider the motivation effects of change on teams. Unfortunately, team leaders have often had little or no training in how to motivate teams; they are expected to pick it up along the way.

In motivating for change where a team structure is involved the following factors are important.

Communication

Changes must be communicated to the teams clearly. The effect on the corporate structure that the changes will make must be clearly described. Discussion and debate are themselves highly motivational, and help to build trust.

Training

Training in change programmes is set out in detail in Chapter 10. Clearly, a highly trained team is a highly motivated one. Individuals in the team must feel competent to do the jobs they will be given by the changes that they are being offered.

Resources

The changes that are being made must be supported by management in tangible ways; there must be adequate back-up of money, people, equipment, authorisations and time. The resources that are available will represent the commitment of management to the changes, and further support the change programme in the eyes of those affected by it.

MOTIVATION AND REWARD

People are only motivated if they feel that there is a reasonable chance that their efforts will lead to obtaining some desired reward or goal. Motivation will take place if the prize offered is valued by the person and there is a good chance of gaining it.

Change agents must remember, when seeking motivation, that there is a direct relationship between the actions and behaviour of an individual and the value that the individual puts on the perceived outcome.

Three important questions should be answered prior to commencing to try to motivate people towards change.

1. What type of expectations does the individual have concerning the work environment?
2. What type of linkages does the individual employee perceive as existing between different types of behaviours at work and the outcomes of those behaviours?
3. What does the individual value?

The expectations individual employees have at any one time can be influenced; as can the perceived linkages between behaviour at work and the consequences of that behaviour. Exerting influence, or trying to exert influence, on what people value during any motivation attempt is difficult. But it can be argued that the discovery and provision of what individuals value in the work environment is an area that has yet to be fully explored by UK organisations.

We believe this can be argued because companies have demonstrated a (wrong) belief that if they address the collective needs of the work-force everyone will respond equally. We have spoken to many managers who have shown that that is their attitude, and have expressed initial surprise when we have asked what they have done to seek out the values of individual members of their staff or teams. The fact that some managers do not even *know* if a team member likes certain sports, or in some cases even if their staff are married, suggests that too little emphasis is put on 'personal' matters. If so little is understood, how can real motivation take place?

As to how this problem can be overcome: team leaders and managers should discover pertinent personal attributes as part of personal development plans and appraisal systems in our organisations. We have always encouraged this in our consultancies.

Up to now there has been a total preoccupation with individual rewards over which most managers and team leaders have little or no control; such as salaries and bonuses. In addition we have often been persuaded that money is what employees value most. Managers and team leaders who agree with this idea, but have little or no control over employees' remuneration, sometimes wrongly come to the conclusion that the organisation stops them from being able effectively to motivate their team members.

BARRIERS TO MOTIVATION

If a barrier is placed in the way of the incentive or reward, then frustration will prevent the person from being motivated. These barriers are often a lack of, or withdrawal of, resources necessary to do the job.

The change programme must anticipate these barriers and dismantle them. Some of the barriers are real, and some are only perceived. However the effect is much the same and open communication will remove the doubts where fears are unfounded.

There can be both tangible and intangible barriers to motivation.

1. Intangible barriers
- Lack of senior management's commitment to the programme of change.
- Close adherence to out-of-date working practices in the belief that they are written in stone.
- Acting and behaving in a way that fails to recognise the needs of the work-force.
- Failing to communicate the proper levels of authority to people.
- Using history and what has gone before as an excuse to find reasons why change will not work.

2. Tangible barriers
- Social and environmental constraints.
- Out-of-date, worn-out and poorly-maintained plant and equipment.
- Poor working conditions.
- Bad relationships with management, staff, work-force, suppliers and customers.
- Lack of people and lack of suitable training.
- Indecision by management.
- Time-management constraints.
- Too low a level of authorisations for resources.

Change managers must make visible the barriers, discuss them and help to remove them if they want change programmes to be accepted.

BASIC MOTIVATIONAL TECHNIQUES

There are basic rules for motivation that cannot be ignored. Change managers must understand these basic motivational techniques if the changes are to be accepted. Any changes which threaten these basic factors will be strongly resisted.

1. People need to feel valued

- Hold meetings to discuss the progress of the change programme.
- Share and demonstrate an interest in the changes being undertaken.
- Create an atmosphere of co-operation.
- Ensure that each individual understands the importance of his or her contribution to the company's performance.
- Ensure that individuals understand the goals of the organisation and why their contribution matters in a wider perspective, beyond the company.

2. Provide scope for development

- Provide adequate job training in skills and development for those who will be changing roles or jobs.
- Arrange and communicate all internal and external contacts with customers, suppliers and so on.
- Encourage horizontal communications.
- Agree sensible and achievable targets.

3. Recognise achievements

- Praise success within the organisation and, where possible, to the outside world as well.
- Remember to praise as well as criticise.
- Counsel individuals towards their targets.
- Communicate the company's and individuals' results and achievements.

4. Provide challenge

- Establish and communicate mutually agreed objectives.
- Provide authorities and permissions that let people take the maximum responsibility for their own actions.

- Establish a succession plan and the expectation of promotion. Support this by training.
- Allow people the chance to take risks. Do not punish failure, but regard it as a learning experience. Help people to learn from this experience.

To judge how people are responding to change programmes we must examine people's behaviour. Behaviour must be properly understood, because one person's behaviour influences the behaviour of others. (Hence the term 'behaviour breeds behaviour'.) Generally, in business, the only part of a person that we see *is* their behaviour.

In most circumstances we can choose the way in which we behave. This is a tool we can use to influence and motivate people around us. By demonstrating confidence in the change process management can encourage acceptance of change in others.

Change managers can, and should, point out to others where their behaviour is in direct conflict with the change programme. This is a difficult process because people often have long-established behavioural patterns, or habits, which up to now have led them to operate in a successful way.

The individual must be encouraged to take a very close, inward look at him or herself to examine his or her own current needs and how these needs are, or are not, being satisfied through the behavioural patterns now being pursued. Obviously it is often the case that those behavioural patterns now being exhibited do not produce outcomes which satisfy the individual's needs because there have now been changes in the work-place.

Change managers must:

- recognise what beliefs are important to them and what goals they want to achieve;
- determine what effects inducements and coercions have on the work-force;
- deal with situations in a positive way;
- identify with the people affected with the changes – 'stepping into their shoes' will demonstrate their fears to you.

Push styles

The above list provides guidelines to the position you are starting from when you are trying to influence motivational behaviour. It should be remembered that many persuasive styles such as the 'carrot' or the 'stick' will achieve short-term acceptance, but if persuasion is achieved through a more open and enlightened route then often a deeper and more committed behaviour will ensue.

'Carrot' and 'stick' methods of making people do things are not motivational, and are part of the push style of influencing behaviour, forcing people to act in a certain way. Such styles move people rather than motivate them. They create a win or lose situation and are only appropriate for obtaining a quick result, i.e. to deal with a crisis.

Typical push styles include threats of authority, aggression, nagging, and pressurising and manipulation. They would normally include short-term bribery and so on.

They create a position of losing face; 'victims' will often seek revenge. As we have already said, people feel insulted to be offered bribes, especially when they know that the money on offer bears no comparison to the effort undertaken. Money should be a recognition of achievement, not a bribe towards that achievement.

Pull styles

Influencing through a pull style is motivational. Pull styles create a situation where someone wants to perform certain tasks. Pull styles must be used sincerely and not in a manipulative or dishonest manner. Used correctly, pull styles lead to a committed effort, and they are morale building. Pull styles create vision, and lead to higher quality performance and challenge in the organisation. It is possibly slower to achieve results with this style because of the element of longer term commitment required through meaningful debate, challenge and thought, but once in place it is more difficult to dislodge the results. Pull styles demand certain ways of behaving and require personal disclosures such as 'I have a problem and I need your help' on the part of management. This invariably means that there must be openness and management must display honesty in its dealings.

Pull styles allow responsibility, project ownership and commitment on the part of others. They include giving recognition and praise, and a demonstration of enthusiasm by management.

Remember, though, that you cannot first use a push style and then hope to apply a pull style. The unenlightened attitudes, the win–lose situation and the lack of commitment of push styles means that you cannot then hope to repair the damage caused.

CHECK LIST OF MOTIVATIONAL FORCES

1. People behave in anticipation of positive reward. Such rewards should therefore always be based on performance and given as soon as possible after the desired performance. Remember that what motivates one person may not necessarily motivate another.
2. Eliminate unnecessary threats and punishments; they only lead to and encourage avoidance behaviour, especially team avoidance.
3. Make sure that accomplishment is adequately recognised. All people need to feel important, no matter how modest their position in the organisation.
4. Provide people with flexibility and choice, empower them and permit employees to make decisions. People who are not given the opportunity to choose for themselves tend to become passive and lethargic.
5. Provide support when it is needed. Employees should be encouraged to ask for support and assistance. Asking for help should not be considered to be a sign of weakness.
6. Provide people with responsibility along with accountability. Few people will reject accountability as long as the tasks in question are within their areas of responsibility and their skill base. They will enjoy accountability if it represents a 'pat on the back' for their efforts.
7. Encourage people to set their own goals or at least to participate actively in the goal-setting process. Accept failures as a

learning process. To 'punish' failure even by intolerant body language (see 12 below) encourages people not to take risks; and risks are essential to creativity.

8. Make sure that employees are aware of how their tasks relate to the organisational goals. Routine work can result in passivity and boredom unless people are aware of how these tasks contribute to the goals of the organisation as a whole.

9. Make sure that people understand your expectations.

10. Allow staff to experience the satisfaction of doing an appropriately challenging job well.

11. Consider your verbal behaviour. Use people's individual names, encourage them to have their say and express their views.

12. Consider your non-verbal behaviour. Adopt an open and relaxed posture, and smile when dealing with staff. Look directly at them when speaking and maintain good eye contact at all times. Use facial expressions to emphasise certain points and do not be afraid to gesture, taking care, of course, to avoid offensive gestures. Where appropriate, inject humour into the situation.

13. Provide people with feedback. This is crucial to their development and must be handled correctly. (There are guidelines to giving feedback below.)

14. Recognise and eliminate barriers to individual achievement.

15. Exhibit confidence in your staff. People who are expected to achieve their new tasks following the change programme will do so more frequently than those who are expected to fail.

16. Encourage people to participate in making decisions that affect them. People who have no control over their destiny become passive, viewing the control of their lives as external to themselves. This can result in learned helplessness.

17. Establish a climate of trust and open communication.

18. People must recognise that their tasks are related to the output of the organisation.

19. Listen to and deal effectively with people's fears.

20. Point out improvements in performance frequently during the early stages of the change programme.

21. Anxiety is fundamental to motivation. The total elimination of

task-anxiety can result in lethargy; however, very high anxiety can result in disorientation and ineffectiveness.

22. Be concerned with short-term and long-term motivation. People who receive only short-term reinforcement and incentives tend to fall short of optimal motivation. They will tend to lack a long-term perspective.

GUIDELINES FOR GIVING FEEDBACK

1. Your description of events should be unambiguous, accurate and should concentrate on facts.
2. Avoid criticism that is not constructive or helpful towards improving a desired result.
3. Comment on areas that individuals can change, such as behaviour.
4. Give feedback in 'bite-sized' chunks; do not overwhelm people. Give people the feedback they can use, and not just the amount needed to 'get it off your chest'.
5. First, tell individuals of their good work and successes, then move on to the weaker aspects that need improvement. Then your comments will not be seen as wholly negative or critical.
6. Ask for reactions to your comments.
7. People are only visible through their behaviour; therefore by communicating about behaviour individuals become aware of areas they can change and improve. .
8. Address the behaviour and not the person. (Say 'There were errors in the work' rather than 'Mike makes a lot of mistakes'.)
9. Restrict the feedback to observations rather than possible conclusions. Conclusions may be wrong-headed; observations accurately noted cannot be.
10. Do not judge. Instead allow self-judgement in discussion.
11. Make feedback relevant by attributing it to specific times and places rather than making general comments.
12. Make feedback a time to share feelings and build solutions, rather than a 'one-way' street for giving comments.

13. Consider the alternative views of the person to whom you are giving feedback.
14. Check with the person that they have understood what you are saying by encouraging them to paraphrase your comments back to you.

II

MAKING
CHANGE
HAPPEN

9

A PROGRAMME FOR CHANGE

Change in organisations can be both proactive and reactive. Obviously proactive change is the preferred course, creating as it does a feeling of being one step ahead of the game. However, most change is reactive; the organisation has to change for identifiable commercial, social or legislative reasons. Although change may be forced upon an organisation due to, say, the necessity for cost cutting leading to organisational restructuring, the acquisition and adopting of new technology, or takeovers and mergers, a programme for change must always be drawn up by management.

Our involvement in major change projects worldwide, some lasting two years from planning to implementation, has borne out the old adage that there is no substitute for planning with change projects. Although we are not identifying particular work done for any individual clients, the major changes we have most recently been involved with include: several programmes for the London Stock Exchange; the introduction of a robotic warehousing and distribution system for a famous Knightsbridge store; assisting in the implementation, through training, of BP Chemicals' cultural change programme 'Towards 2000'; total quality management (TQM) for BP Chemicals and Barclays Global Securities; preparing for change with COHSE prior to their amalgamation with NUPE and NALGO; assisting in the introduction of retail outlets in France for New Look, a leading women's fashion house.

Successful change demands total involvement and commitment from everybody in the organisation, whether they are going to be affected by the change or not.

STAGE ONE – OUTLINE PLAN

The first stage is for senior management to draw up an outline plan for change for presentation to general management. Although there are no blueprints for such outline plans, the following can be recommended as a starting point. Obviously these points can be customised by change managers to suit their particular needs.

1. The reasons for change, the planning and implementation of the change project, and how such a programme fits with the overall strategy of the organisation (or that part of the organisation that is going to be affected)

Although it is not currently popular to talk of 'vision' in organisations, change is only accepted when everyone involved has a view of the big picture: what is going to change, when is it going to change, how will the changes affect people, how does this change benefit the business? This outline sketch should be sufficient to focus management's attention, but flexible enough to enable management to fill in the details. Everyone thereby becomes, quite correctly, part of the planning process, taking full ownership of the programme. The culture of the organisation will determine the degree of openness that senior management feel that they can communicate in the plans. The rule of change is, if in doubt, over-communicate. Even if the overcommunication leads to embarrassment later on at least it will bring issues into the open. Through consultation and debate, serious matters of potential conflict can be addressed at this early stage.

2. The identification of those people who will be affected by the change programme

What often happens is that by the time senior management agree to the planning of change they have already accepted the need for it and have taken ownership of it themselves. Because of this they usually assume that everybody else in the organisation will see the sense of what they wish to do. They often forget that execution of the plan is not participative management. As a generalisation, in any organisation change will affect everybody, though some people will be affected more than others. In some change programmes the people who are going to be affected stand out and can therefore be consulted, and some people will be unaffected and can be dealt with accordingly. The problem area usually concerns large numbers of people where it is not known how the change will affect them.

For example, in a recent change programme we discovered that new technology was leading to job losses. The organisation's culture had steadily been moving from an autocratic, secretive culture to an empowering and more open culture. This naturally led to staff asking who were to be the stayers and who the leavers. Management could not answer this question in terms of names, only in terms of numbers. In this particular situation we had some sympathy with senior management as they appeared to be in a no-win situation. All they could promise to do was to identify who would be staying as quickly as possible. In the meantime the uncertainty that this caused increased staff's resistance to the other, smaller changes as they were introduced.

With careful planning, however, some of these problems could have been avoided. The new technology, although radical in its scope, and the impact it would have upon the industry, was basically simple in operation. Management, together with the personnel department, should have identified those people with the necessary skills quite quickly, instead of being distracted by more high-profile 'fancy' projects. Stayers and leavers could then be assured of their position and the uncertainty put to rest.

As we said, shocking though redundancy is, the fear of it is often more destructive to people than the impact.

3. A comparison of pre-change and post-change organisation structures

Most people like the order and stability which enables them to get on with their jobs and satisfy their basic organisational needs. Change represents uncertainty; it is known often to produce individual repositioning within the organisational structure (promotion, demotion, transfers that are welcome and some that are not). One of the comfort factors that change managers can give their staff is some indication of where they will fit into the new structure. Unfortunately this is, in practice, very difficult to do at the planning stage of a change programme. However, this does not mean that it should not be done as effectively as possible in the circumstances. It is normally a matter of communication and consultation. Organigrams (mini organisation charts) are used as signposts in the change process and must be discussed with staff.

All too often during a change programme management indulge themselves in the full-time operation of drawing up organisation charts, forgetting to involve others. For example, in one retail organisation with which we worked, new organigrams were issued every Friday afternoon. The impact upon morale in that business was, predictably, rather disturbing.

All change has to be reflected in a structural sense otherwise it may not happen at all. The post-change organisation chart should be kept as fluid, and as open, as possible so that when issues arise all those involved in the change process can be part of the decision-making process. Everyone has their role to play in the crafting of the eventual structure.

4. Outline the analysis of the impact of the changes on the stakeholders, i.e. shareholders, customers, suppliers, bankers, staff and the local community

Take into account the effect of new technology and updated processes upon the industry at large. Even the monopolies, such as privatised water, electricity, gas and telecommunications companies, have to take account of the wishes of government regulatory authorities. In modern times organisations are not islands; in fact the much heralded '1992' European Community move from 'Island' to 'European' mentality with the Single European Market has been a major change programme in itself.

All change within any organisation will have an impact upon the following:

Shareholders

Shareholdings have increased with privatisations and increased investments through life assurance, endowment schemes and pension schemes. Changes to an organisation may affect the shareholders' view of the organisation; for instance, companies heavily involved in polluting the atmosphere or exploiting ethnic races in other countries may find it increasingly difficult to raise money in the capital markets.

At the present time the most forceful of these voices are politically motivated; banks have had to withdraw activity from South Africa as anti-apartheid feeling increased. In the future we may see environmental concerns creating similar pressures, though they have not quite succeeded yet. We are seeing, however, the emergence of unit trusts for those who wish to invest only in 'green' companies. That trend could accelerate as the unit trust companies show that they are proactive to change pressures.

Customers

Customers are more aware of choice and quality issues than ever before. The effects of change need careful examination through the customer microscope. Like shareholders, customers are increasingly aware of environmental issues as well as traditional concerns like 'value for money'.

One of the greatest changes facing customers (i.e. individuals) is that they are now being presented with health and education on a consumer basis. What used to be State-given is now, it seems, given reluctantly; customers have to 'shop around' for their services.

The customer is, however, being recognised in other ways by the government. Prime Minister John Major's 'Citizen's Charter' is designed to recognise the voices of those who have little clout against bigger organisations. The Charter has, however, been dismissed as a vote-catching gimmick; it is in its early days and time will tell if it has real ability. At the end of September 1992 the first awards were presented based on this philosophy.

The first 36 Charter Marks were awarded to schools, hospitals, government agencies, local authority services, privatised utilities, police services and one prison. The aim of the Charter is, to quote 'Citizen's Charter First Report 1992':

> to make sure that if mistakes are made, they are put right quickly. Every Charter issued now explains how and where people can complain. Many services are revising their complaints procedures to make them easier to use and understand.

There are now 28 Charters covering patients, parents, passengers, council tenants, benefits agency customers, job seekers, court users and others.

Suppliers

Change may lead to reassessments of the company-to-supplier interface; purchasing for profit may lead to new suppliers or revising existing contractual arrangements. Change towards total quality management (TQM) has had a profound impact upon relationships with suppliers.

For example, Marks and Spencer have long pioneered partnerships with their suppliers. They have assured them that they will prefer them and will not seek alternatives, in return for a commitment to quality. They have observed their rules rigidly with a positive end result for the customer – Marks and Spencer have an enviable reputation for quality.

Bankers

Bankers and other suppliers of capital are also affected by change. Banks, so they say, 'lend to the man, not to the security' (on the other hand, they make sure they get the security under their belts while they say it!). Most bankers are therefore lending not just to the company but to the whole management team. If, due to a change programme, that management team is altered then the organisation has a duty to keep bankers and investors informed. Arguably, that duty includes perhaps making the banks themselves part of the change process through consultation.

Staff

Most captains of industry are on record as stating that staff are their most valuable asset and change normally affects those assets most of all. It is necessary, therefore, and of the utmost importance, to monitor the effect of change upon the staff. If possible, parallel change projects should be monitored to see what effect the change programme had in the final analysis.

However rough, an outline impact analysis upon the staff can be thought through. It just takes research and perhaps the use of outside consultants who have worked in change projects in similar industries. A modern example has been the effect of new technology on the financial services industries; there have been lessons in the effects on staff that can be used to assist in similar change projects.

The local community

Since the middle of the 1960s, in the UK, there has been increasing awareness of the effect of major change upon local communities. Unfortunately, economic expedience is still witness to the punishing effect change can have. The restructuring of British Coal and British Steel produced examples of whole towns being economically wiped out through large-scale closure. The so-called 'peace dividend', the result of the end of the Cold War and the break up of the Eastern bloc is deeply affecting our defence industries, with a knock-on effect on local communities.

For instance, in September 1992 British Aerospace, in Hatfield north of London, laid off 2000 of the work-force and closed the site. A further 1000 jobs were lost from other sites. Since the end of the Cold War in 1990, 43,000 jobs have been lost from the defence industry, devastating local communities where skilled and unskilled alike are unable to find replacement work.

New technologies and processes

The free market mentality compels us to acknowledge that gaining a competitive edge through the introduction of new technologies and processes is acceptable. The dilemma here for change managers is that we are also forced to take not just a free market viewpoint, but also a national viewpoint and now even a European one. This issue brings into play social and economic arguments which must be considered.

5. Budgets

Change programmes are normally expensive. We only have to look at the reports and accounts, and the financial statements of any organisation that has undergone or is going through a change process to see the cost of change. These costs are usually shown as restructuring costs or extraordinary items of expenditure. Because of the nature of change, which is often an evolutionary process, most managements are timid when it comes to costing the programme. However, the programme must be costed and the payback periods calculated at sensible rates of interest.

All change programmes should be treated like any other form of capital or revenue expenditure. A favourite 'trick' of management is to charge the costs of the change to existing budgets under the theory (or excuse) that change is self-financing. This is nonsense in major reorganisations where the restructuring costs, including redundancies and plant or shop closures, are immense and cannot be assimilated within existing allocations. There must be a separate change programme budget and all change managers must have taken part in its construction.

Analysis of the competencies of management to execute the change programme

This is a difficult matter for management to address as it involves some very honest self-assessment as to whether or not as individuals, or as part of a team, they feel able to execute the change programme. For this reason major change projects are often reasons for resignation; some genuine and some of the 'Did he fall or was he pushed?' variety. In the newspapers we read of boardroom splits or the removal of a chief executive and their direct followers because they are now out of step with their colleagues. The competence of management to change is attitudinal and behavioural rather than a challenge to the technical or interpersonal skills of the individual managers concerned.

Because change is instigated and driven from the top it is essential that senior management sign up to the change. Honest management will debate the issues out and then either 'buy into' the change programme or leave the organisation. There can be extraordinary damage to change programmes done by managers who 'sit on the fence' and wait to see 'which way the wind is blowing'.

In 1992, in one of Britain's largest multinational companies, the chief executive was encouraged to stand down by pressure from the non-executive directors. This particular chief executive had initiated probably the most radical change, company-wide, that the organisation had seen in its long history. He had no doubt been part of the process that appointed some of his fellow executive and non-executive directors. When he resigned his was the only resignation. Did this mean that the change he had started would now be ditched or did it mean that the change programme was sound, but that he was not the person to lead it?

In any change programme, what really matters is that senior management carefully consider if they are truly confident to see the change through. They must also be sure of their own competencies.

7. Identification of the driving forces and the restraining forces which will facilitate the change programme

Although a more in-depth analysis of driving and restraining forces is examined in Chapters 5 and 6, any change project must address those issues that would drive the change project forward and those matters that will naturally hinder its progress. Obviously any management team with the right experience will intuitively understand the driving and restraining forces prevalent in the organisation. It must be remembered that these will vary from one company to another, and that there are geographical and regional variations due to the history of local communities. The use and evaluation of case studies and the use of external consultants will be invaluable here. If interventions are used – such as bonus and loyalty payments – to decrease the restraining forces, they must be used with care, since they lose their effect if kept in place too long (see Chapter 8). The increase of driving forces and the decrease of restraining forces can usually be addressed in the training room, using open discussion groups to bring fears, wants and needs into the open, and by formulating plans to address the natural resistance to change.

8. The setting up of a small but flexible team whose responsibility will be to drive the change forward

Although we have always stressed that change is initiated from the top, change cannot be delegated down the line because to do so will ensure failure. Resistance to change is strongest at the middle management level. These senior managers very rarely see the necessity for change and hide behind the belief that they know what they are doing, why they are there and that they have worked hard to get there. They also know where they want to go. For these reasons change is a threat to their ambitions and sense of order; in many organisations these middle managers have successfully killed off many change initiatives.

For these reasons the setting up of a change task-force is essential.

This task-force should be removed from day-to-day line responsibilities and, although small in number, it should enthusiastically co-opt members for specific issues. The following guidelines will be useful when setting up task-forces.

- The task-force should consist of representatives from all the major departments and divisions.
- The chairperson should be impartial, preferably an external change consultant or a senior member of the organisation with no department or divisional responsibilities.
- The task-force should have total budgetary control.
- It should have the authority to co-opt any member of the organisation for varying periods of time.
- It should report directly to the chief executive.
- It should publish its findings, progress, successes and failures on a routine, regular basis to all members of the organisation.
- It should have the authority within its budgets for inter-company and organisational visits. This allows for cross-pollination of the best practices in other companies.
- Each member of the task-force should be assured of his or her position in the organisation. It is essential that those people can concentrate their energy on the work in hand and be totally impartial in the execution of their duties.
- When the change programme is complete the task-force should self-destruct and not try to keep itself in existence.

9. The time plan

From our experience too many organisations do not spend enough time calculating the time frame of the programme. However difficult and unrealistic it may be at the outset, time planning is of the utmost importance. A programme for change, like any other corporate project, must identify its key dates and milestones. Change programmes are just normal, large-scale projects and subject to the usual 'rules' of project management. Achievable deadlines must be communicated down the line. The task-force's job is to ensure continuity and the meeting of deadlines; staff will accept change more readily when they have a start and finish date. Too many change projects never seem to end; rather they evolve into an unnecessary fine-tuning vehicle to allow management to keep fiddling with the process.

A popular game now played by management is to roll one change programme into another. This is the so-called 'seamless tapestry theory', which is possibly exciting for senior management but very disconcerting to the staff who see the seams and the patchiness of the programme at the local level all too easily.

10. Communications

In any change programme it is essential to set up a communication structure so that every member of the organisation knows where to go to find out what is happening. There are a variety of ideas on how best to develop communication channels. The most unimaginative merely adhere to the existing communication channels, i.e. down the line and through the work-force and staff representatives. We often recommend the introduction of an 'ombudsman' who reports to the chief executive and is completely independent of the change task-force and line management. The most successful candidates for such a post are strong managers who are possibly near retirement age. This ensures impartiality and corporate independence. The ombudsman should have the authority to collect information from the board, the task-force, and the staff and workforce. If possible, he or she should issue a periodic newssheet explaining the issues and resolutions. The ombudsman should not be treated as a court of appeal, but more as a legal friend to all parties.

▌STAGE TWO – SUBMITTING THE PLAN

The second stage of the programme for change is to submit the outline plan to the divisions and all departments, and to start the consultation process with front-line management unions, staff consultancy committees and team leaders. We know that change is most easily achieved when those affected are fully consulted in the change programme, so at this stage in the plan it is essential to make the key players part of the planning process. The outline plan should therefore now be given to middle management with the brief that, through consultation, local issues should now be addressed. The localised change programme should be concerned with the following.

1. The necessity for the change programme, how it has arisen and how it will impact upon the division or department concerned

By reducing the level of abstraction from the big (overview) picture to departmental issues, management will gain a greater understanding of the problems, fears and restraints that will have to be faced when it comes to implementation. There is a tendency at this stage for the process to get too trivial, reaching a level of detail that is not only unnecessary but increasingly boring to third parties. But it is necessary for people to have their say, let off steam and feel involved. The reactions to the overall plan should, of course, be fed to the task-force who can then begin to collate responses.

2. The 'people plan'

Because eventually, in some way or another, everyone in the organisation will be affected by the changes, it is essential in the local plan to start calculating the 'people plan', i.e. those who will be staying, leaving, those for reassignment and those for retraining. It is also essential that all staff realise and appreciate that it is their own team leader or management that is doing this evaluation. Management cannot opt out of this process by shifting responsibility to senior management or to a task-force. This is not to say that the staff will not be resistant to change just because their own manager is instrumental in it, but human nature still leads us to prefer hearing news of our health from our own GP rather than in an anonymous letter from the General Medical Council.

It is worth pointing out here that in many successful change projects we have noticed that there has been a significant willingness of people to accept voluntary redundancy. For example, during British Telecom's 1992 restructuring they sought around 25,000 voluntary redundancies and received over four times that number of volunteers. From our experience voluntary redundancy is best addressed at the local level rather than through a central personnel function. The job of central personnel is to calculate the terms of voluntary redundancy rather than control the whole process.

3. Change agents

Middle management should now identify those key members of staff who will be part of the planning process and those who will be members of the implementation teams, i.e. the change agents we refer to in Chapter 11. These key members of the change process should be those people who have demonstrated an aptitude for change, as well as some who at this stage are resistant to change. Successful change cannot be achieved by only 'the good guys'; it is necessary to involve the bad guys, the cynics and those who openly state that they have 'seen it all before'. The anti-change people, if made part of the plan in an implementation process, will make vocal and visible those issues that are worrying the staff and the work-forces. In their own way they are leaders who are putting forward the viewpoints of the resistance movement. They fulfil a necessary and useful function. It should also be pointed out that, in our experience, after debate and analysis of the issues, such people often end up the strongest champions of change in the long run.

4. Names in boxes

At this local stage managers can now – through consultation – begin to put the names in the boxes so that local organigrams can be constructed department by department. The results can be fed back to the task-force for co-ordination and evaluation. They will be ensuring that there are no duplications of functions and so on. This involvement in the local planning level is essential for both staff and work-force to demonstrate that their own local management are in control of the process and not merely servants of a faceless body.

5. Evaluation of the budget

The task-force, we have recommended, has ownership of the change budget. However, in practice there must be an evaluation of the budget examining the overall sum from the bottom up. Within the financial guidelines, department or divisional managers – in consultation with their staff – can now draw up the detailed financial statements of what is necessary to drive the change forward. Below is a list of suggestions for local management to cost:

- inter-company visits;
- training for new technology and general management training;
- redundancy costs (both forced and voluntary);
- other closure costs;
- costs of new plant and equipment, updated kit, computer software etc.;
- 'people' costs, including recognition parties, special bonuses, etc. There will need to be rewards for meeting successful milestones.

6. Local impact analysis

In the outline plan we considered impact analysis upon the stakeholders. This can now be thrashed out to a detail of local knowledge by those who, in particular, will have a more detailed knowledge of the possible impact upon customers, suppliers, staff, work-force and so on. This can mean that the task-force receives a combination of both correct and biased information. By comparing this information with the information from other sections of the organisation, partisan buyers and favouritism can be weeded out. Because people are involved in this information-gathering process, they will feel that their special relationships with customers, suppliers and others, are not being ignored. As the staff and work-force also live in the local communities it is essential to get their views as to what the change will mean to the non-employees of the organisation. From our experience in large factories and plants we have found that if we can sell the change programme to our own staff (who are often our own worst critics), then we can sell it to the community at large.

7. Middle and junior managers as drivers of change

Regarding management competence, it is now necessary to consider the ability of middle management and junior management to drive the change process. As we have stated, middle management are normally the most resistant to change. From their point of view they have often got the most to lose. For that reason they must not be put in a position where they are able to block the change process. They must, of course, be given time to change within the guidelines of the time plan, but eventually they must either come on board or be removed from the organisation.

From our experience resistance is not always a function of age; many people seem to believe that the older a manager is the more resistant to change he or she will be. We have found age to be irrelevant, indeed some of the youngest managers fresh out of college or university with, say, two years' front-line experience, are often the nearest to Luddites.

Unfortunately we can only encourage change, we cannot force it. Change that is forced loses its effect when the driving forces, i.e. more money and other driving forces that we may put in place, are removed. Training (examined in Chapter 10) can help, but all too often in major change projects it is not possible to win everybody round. In these instances we strongly recommend that those who are inflexible be relocated to an area where their resistance to change is muted. They generally leave the organisation in the long run.

8. Redefine driving and restraining forces

However time-consuming and tedious, it will be necessary to redefine and rechallenge the driving and restraining forces at the local level. While a new company car may be a driving force for a divisional director, a mere parking place may be the driving force for the stores assistant. While not encouraging bitching sessions it will be necessary – always through group discussions and brainstorming sessions – to work out the drivers and restrainers for change. Such sessions reveal the common threads running through many organisations, together with the minor concerns that have been allowed to fester over the years. So often these 'oddities' represent an exaggerated but real piece of the change puzzle.

9. Time objectives

The overall time frame has been set in the outline plan by senior management. These dates are properly known as the time objectives. The local plan will have to translate these key dates into achievable pieces of work with very clear objectives. The information coming from the local plans, as co-ordinated by the task-force, must not be allowed to alter the overall time frame, but the local issues raised will pinpoint where resources will have to be allocated to meet the plan. Failing to do that would be allowing slippage; and the milestones and key dates would appear to be not so critical. The local time plan is, of course, the project control for the local staff involved. The local plan would also pinpoint initial areas of resistance to staff plans, the introduction of new technology and training plans.

STAGE THREE – CO-ORDINATING LOCALISED PLANS INTO THE INITIAL PLAN

The third and final stage is to co-ordinate the localised plans into the initial plan. This, then, becomes the master plan. It is at this stage that the bottom-up process can now be commissioned. Consultation must continue to go right down the line; there are many instances, especially with regard to staffing levels, training and the introduction of new plant and equipment, where we can, and should, now take advice from the people who have to deal with the changes, i.e. our staff and our work-force. This can be done through briefing meetings in quality work groups, where these are already in existence. The bottom-up initiatives and consultation should include the following points.

- The reason why management have embarked upon the change process and the possible outcomes, both good and bad, to the individuals and teams concerned.
- The necessity of getting everyone on site involved in the process and working to the same end. This despite the fact that some of the individuals may be positively or adversely affected by the change programme.
- An explanation of how managers see the new organisation structure, at the same time encouraging, if not overtly demanding, their local input. It must be stressed that organisation charts are not written in stone and can be negotiated.
- A detailed description of what is necessary to bring the change process about. The briefing meetings which are held for items such as vision and corporate strategy are important, but often relevant to only a few. Large-scale change is the sum of little changes; it is these little changes that are of interest to all the staff.

The setting out of plans for more complex change programmes can often be aided with the use of diagrams. These may also be an easier way of communicating complex plans to others. We suggest that the reader faced with complex planning should turn to Chapter 15 to see the two most useful forms of diagram available as tools of such planning and communication.

10

TRAINING FOR CHANGE

The roles of training, the training department, and the training management and staff have changed significantly in most major organisations during the 1980s. Managers and staff have had to acquire many new skills. The main reasons for this have been the rapid introduction of new technologies, change initiatives such as total quality management and the customer focus programmes. Modern managers are living in a changing and volatile environment. The new driving forces for training in organisations are therefore different to those of the 1980s, but unfortunately the majority of our training departments and training managers are still living in that world. This makes it difficult for them to develop programmes for change, or indeed to train for change. This chapter identifies what needs to change to bring trainers up to speed, and to increase the return on the organisations' training expenditures.

Changing technologies have increased the speed at which we are having to train employees. In order to manage the new technologies in an increasingly turbulent environment, we must train everybody in the new working methods and new organisational structures that are necessary to maximise their effectiveness. For this reason we are having to train people to accept not just new procedures and equipment, but training people to accept cultural change itself. In fact, change is now so rapid that people undergoing changing environments need 'counselling'; a major part of what training for change involves.

COMMITMENT FROM THE TOP

The training function in any organisation is only as good as the support it receives from the senior management. The increasing status and impact of professional human resources management in many companies has influenced – for the good – the attitudes of top executives. Although many companies state that training is a function of line management it is now accepted that the success of training programmes reflects the competence of training managers, and their ability to 'sell' their programmes to senior and line management.

One of the most common complaints from staff is that senior management do not seem committed to training. This is not an idle complaint; it is often evidenced by withdrawing delegates from training courses at short notice, refusing requests for training courses, cutting back training budgets in times of recession and taking no active interest in the training that staff have received. Since many senior executives are on record as stating that 'people are our most important asset', they might try to show and demonstrate that commitment by supporting the training throughout the organisation. This often means that senior management itself must change and accept the following guidelines.

- Senior management must accept that training is one of the main drivers of the business and allocate sufficient funds to that end.
- Training departments, until recently often seen as a house of correction and a semi-retirement home for tired managers and staff, must be seen as being essential to the organisation's strategic goals.
- Management and staff development should move from a 'nice to do' position to being part of the business strategy. One of our client companies used to have no training strategy at all; they

would contact us and ask when we could do some training and then they would 'find a few bodies to put on whatever course we thought we could hold'. Over a period of time we were able to convince them that this just was not training in the real sense. Now they have a forward plan of training for at least a year ahead, and their staff know in advance what co-ordinated training they will be receiving. Of course, the employees have all had input into that training plan, making their involvement more committed and the training more a part of the organisational goals.

- Human resource departments must be empowered to make a contribution to the 'bottom line' by recruiting talented people, training them and developing them. They should not let people stagnate on the job, or end their days disillusioned with a company that they originally joined with enthusiasm and great expectations.

- Senior management, in times of recession, must learn not to wipe out training departments or habitually cut back on training, but must expand it instead. They should use periods of slow growth to retrain staff to use the new technologies and new ways of working. The companies that succeed after recessions are those that have maintained the primary asset of their people.

- Senior management must allocate time to allow themselves to be part of the training effort. They should welcome the opportunity to take part in training sessions rather than making it a totally delegated function, or one they are prepared to suffer if there is 'nothing much else to do'.

TECHNOLOGICAL CHANGE

No company, division, department, section, manager or employee is immune from the impact of new technology. Historically, people have always had to change; accept new kit, machines, tools and so on, but they have never had to accept it at the speed we are presently seeing. There is no indication that the pace will slow and every indication that it will continue to increase.

Because of that pace it is no longer possible to train people in technological change 'going down the ranks'. Senior managers have had to learn to use personal computers, while their own first-line managers are doing the same thing. The impact of these technologies is also changing job descriptions: for example, in one organisation we know of the role of the first-line manager has changed from spending 80 per cent of his or her time on the shop floor to, over a three-year period, less than 20 per cent. A great deal of his or her time is now spent running the department through a computer keyboard.

By far the greatest impact of technological change for the training department is that non-managerial staff are now in the front line for training. Until around the 1970s a trained person from whatever discipline (such as a secretary, a tool maker, a cab driver) could ply his or her trade safe in the knowledge that, whatever changes arose, they would have the time and instructional training to cope. For example, secretaries had time to make the transition from manual to electric typewriters without too much difficulty. However, computer technologies are now replacing electromechanical processes. Typists had to learn to use word processors almost overnight, or become outdated and literally redundant. Waiters even use hand-held information processors; cab drivers use computer communication links. Almost no job has been unaffected by the rapid development of computer technology.

This has meant that our training population has increased, often without the training departments getting the right resources to meet the demand. Furthermore, in the scramble to get trained, people are being put on courses that are not suitable to their personal or business needs.

New products and services

New technology has also accelerated the introduction of new products and services. New products and services used to be introduced in a few cities, market tested for a period of perhaps several years, and then moved out gradually across the country. This allowed for time to train enough people to sell and service the new products, however this is no longer the case.

The gradual introduction of automatic cash dispensers was acceptable in the 1970s and 1980s; any bank or building society introducing a new product or service in this manner today would lose much of its market share to a more dynamic competition. This often means having to train everyone involved before any product or service has even been launched. Inevitably there has to be an emphasis on quality of training; there are fewer opportunities to learn from mistakes.

Proactive training

Training departments, and training programmes, therefore have to be a lot more proactive to the needs of the business than formerly. Therefore, the training function must itself change; we recommend the following.

- Training managers and staff must become more proactive to technological change by keeping up with modern developments, through reading, attending courses and, where possible, using the new technology in operation.
- Where possible, new technology such as IT systems, computers, simulators, model offices or control rooms should be constructed in the training department for hands-on introduction.
- Training programmes and courses should be constructed from scratch, rather than the present method of rehashing an existing programme.
- New technology training should be for small groups of people at similar grades in the organisation. This training should be preceded by an explanation of how the new technology fits into the process and its benefit to the organisation.
- Trainers should be experts with the new technology. For this reason companies should, where necessary, bring in an outside expert to do the training.
- If possible, arrange site, factory or office visits where the new technology has been introduced. Give trainees a chance to talk to the people who operate it, as well as seeing it in action.
- Remember that training is as important as the new technology itself; one cannot succeed without the other.

MANAGEMENT TRAINING

As change in our organisations is managed by the management, a comprehensive review of the state of management training is necessary to see if management are getting the tools to do the job. If managers are not so equipped they will feel unsure of themselves, and this will readily be communicated to the staff and work-force. The sad fact is that in many organisations the management are more frightened of change than most of the employees, for just this reason.

As management trainers we have had many opportunities to influence management training in various types of organisations and have therefore been able to assess the results of front-line management training. Management training is unfortunately often regarded by senior line management as 'that long-haired stuff'. It is treated as 'something we have to do to keep good staff because we promised them such training when we took them on'.

Another common stumbling block is that some managers believe managerial skills cannot be taught, but rather that they are something people learn with experience ('the hard way' in the 'University of Life'). Because of these outdated attitudes most management training amounts to no more than a corporate version of 'keeping up with the Joneses' (i.e. other companies). The training 'programmes' consist only of doing what other companies do ('no more and no less').

In many organisations the only management training on offer is as follows:

- Introduction to Information Technology
- Presentation skills
- Report writing
- Accounts for non-financial managers
- Influencing skills
- Chairing and participation in meetings
- Time management

Empowering training for managers

The above courses and/or workshops are essential development training for all managers so that they can do their job more efficiently and be better able to communicate to all levels of the organisation, customers, suppliers etc. But management training must not stop there. Modern managers, with their particular skills in their chosen field, must, if they are to add value to their job, be taught and given instruction in those areas that will prepare them to lead their staff in an empowered manner. To put it another way, we must give them the skills and confidence to run their own patch as if they owned it. Other useful courses include:

- Teambuilding
- Managing risk
- Work group leader training
- How to develop and introduce a strategy
- How to cost control your own department
- Managing people
- Managing change
- Cultural change
- Organisational change
- Budgeting and financial systems

The above list is not meant to be exhaustive, but it gives an indication of the areas in which the modern manager must be well grounded.

Some companies should also offer an 'Outsourcing transition' course. Many companies do not do all of their work with in-house employees, but outsource it to other firms and individuals. Many of those individuals are drawn from former members of staff. It is not unusual to see people made redundant and then taken back as subcontractors to do much the same work. However, their terms and conditions of 'employment' are very different, and the subcontractor must understand the difference in his or her position. The principal differences are set out in detail in Chapter 13.

External trainers

Management training is also one of the areas where the use of external instructors and training consultants to augment in-house trainers is essential. Most in-house management trainers do a highly professional job but they are limited in their scope of subjects, inexperienced in planning training programmes and their breadth of experience may be limited due to having been with the company for a considerable period. Training consultants should be used as a more cost-effective alternative to internal staffing, and to offer the wider experience and more diverse interests that most training departments cannot offer. Furthermore, the more complex training programmes involve challenging existing corporate boundaries; that simply cannot be done from within.

For similar reasons much more use should be made of the further educational establishments than is done at present. These colleges and universities have the facility and ability to offer competitive courses in core subjects. They have the added advantage of bringing together delegates from other companies and organisations.

Management training is fundamental to managing the change process and we recommend the following.

- Promote management training as part of someone's job description. Do not use it as an ad-hoc add-on for corrective action, or just to fulfil a promise previously made, but which has no substantial company support.
- Differentiate between core skill subjects and the new higher skills managers need to manage their part of the business.
- Management training should be open to all, and should be used for pre-promotion training as well as a catch-up process for newly promoted managers.
- Ideally, management training should not be used as a reward for promotion, but rather as a preparation for it.
- More use should be made of external resources such as colleges and training consultants.
- More effort is needed in the design of current training courses to ensure their effectiveness and relevance.

- Senior line management must demonstrate commitment to the training effort and participate in training courses.
- Delegates must be assured that management training is not a punishment.

CULTURAL CHANGE

Training for cultural change, which we have defined and discussed in previous chapters, is a relatively new area that training departments are having to get to grips with. Changing the culture of an organisation, as we have discussed, is a slow process and cannot be done by management edict. It is a question of inertia; companies and their cultures grow up over a long period of time, and it takes either an equally long period of time or (more realistically) a hugely accelerated effort to 'move the mountain'. As we know, people can – and do – pay lip-service only to the new culture, while remaining totally committed to the old and existing culture. This can mean that over the course of time the old culture will reassert itself with its adherents believing that they may have lost a few initial battles but will win the war.

Some companies have approached cultural change training in some very strange ways. For example, one senior training manager instructed us to 'bone up on the so-called new culture and mention it now and again in existing training courses'. (Lip-service indeed!) Taking the view that the customer is always right and, more seriously, to see what effect this plan of action would have (and to demonstrate effectively that this was not a practical approach), we did exactly as asked. The upshot was total confusion. The trainees, having never heard of the so-called new culture, spent most of the duration of the course trying to find out something about it, and to see what impact it would have upon them. Furthermore it was demotivating because the general 'feeling' was that something bad was being hidden from the work-force. The organisation and the trainers were made to look foolish and unprepared. We then set up a sensible training programme that cured these ills, at least part of our function being to rebuild trust in a management that was, by now, genuinely more enlightened.

In another organisation, we were employed to assist in what can only be described as a 'Cultural Change Crusade Day'. In this particular company the human resources department had agreed with the board of directors a new set of values and goals by which the company was now going to be driven. A day was allocated and we, with senior line management, were asked to hold a series of culture workshops with the instruction: 'Get 'em excited, wind 'em up, get 'em enthused about it, give 'em the brochure and send 'em back to work.' Needless to say the short-term effect was wonderful, but within a month the whole thing had been forgotten. The chances of changing a company culture like this are about as likely as buying a 'play the violin in a day' book and planning to end the evening on stage at the Albert Hall!

The most amusing example of how *not* to do it was the 'creep up on them quietly' approach. In this case, in workshops over six months, management had agreed the cultural changes necessary for the business. They had done so without any representatives of the staff or work-force being present. The plan was that management would lead by example; they would start living the new culture. In other words they would use the new ways of treating the staff and work-force in the anticipation that employees would see this demonstration of the new culture and respond positively to it. What actually happened was that the staff and work-force (as management found out later) realised (assisted by the inevitable 'leaks') what was happening and childishly ignored the new culture for months. Management gave up and considered another approach.

Cultural change training guidelines

From these experiences, and from our current work, we have developed cultural change training guidelines as follows.

- Be bold and proud about your new culture. Tell everyone, i.e. staff, work-force, customers, suppliers etc., what the new culture is all about.
- Train people by holding one-day workshops for teams of up to twenty people, so that they can work through the new culture.

Such workshops should include representatives of senior management, with trainers and consultants acting as facilitators.

- Train everybody in the organisation. This includes contractors, consultants and part-time staff.
- Create large, imaginative visual aids reinforcing the highlights of the new culture. Put them up in prominent places throughout the organisation.
- Encourage people to talk about the new culture in all training sessions, workshops, meetings etc.
- Reward successful application of the new culture with recognition for individuals as well as teams.
- Repeat the workshops with the same teams for half-day sessions three months later. This will let all parties assess and discuss the problems of living in the new culture.
- Appoint, and explain the role of, the change agents whose job it is to counsel about – and drive home – the new culture.

▌STAFF AND WORK-FORCE TRAINING

In all the change projects that we have been involved with, training (both good and bad) has normally been given to all grades of management. But many organisations still avoid the issue of training for change with staff and work-force. The rule of thumb seems to be that change-training is suitable 'for grade X and above', but people below that grade will somehow have to pick it up as they go along. There are probably many historical and current reasons for this type of attitude, but from our experience the more common are as follows (and all are wrong, or merely excuses).

- Line management do not truly believe that staff and the work-force are the prime assets of the business, despite what they may say. They really view them as expendable operatives.
- People below a certain grade are not thought to be receptive to training because they see it as a management trick to get something for nothing.

- When it comes to change programmes people prefer to be led by the nose. They like to be instructed in what to do rather than, through training, working out the issues for themselves.
- Most training departments are not geared up to training the whole of the staff and work-force, and therefore are not proactive in pushing the training down the line.
- Line management feel that most employees have enough problems coping with skills training. To subject them to 'academic teaching' on change issues would lead to learning overload.
- Staff and the work-force are the doers, not the thinkers, and therefore are not comfortable in a training environment.
- Most staff and members of the work-force have been away from any form of formal education for so long that they are incapable of concentrating on the issues. They will merely waste time on the training courses.
- Line management cannot evaluate the payback for the training investment and accordingly cannot usually get top management support.

Because of these outdated and wrong ideas, change-training programmes all too often become a compromise between management and the training department. In too many organisations the change training effort is as follows:

The board and direct reports	one day overview
Senior management	one week residential
Middle management	half week on site
First line management	one/two-day workshops
Staff/work-force	half-day briefing session

As we are often pointing out to our client organisations this training effort is executed in almost exactly the reverse priority to what it should be. It is sensible to argue that the people who will be most affected, and who will actually be making it happen, should get the lion's share of the training.

As we have argued, training for change is as important as the change itself. Staff and work-forces have a right not only to understand what the organisation is doing, but why they are doing it.

Importantly, they must be given the confidence to make the necessary transitions and to seek guidance along the way. The only way this can be done is to give them the same opportunity to understand the process as is given to their managers.

We therefore recommend the following.

- All staff and work-force should be trained in their own teams with their team leader playing a major role.
- Follow-up training and reviews should be done in mixed teams so that problems, successes, fears and developments can be shared; and joint solutions proposed.
- The training should be informal, preferably interactive, and as far removed from classroom instruction as possible.
- People are very receptive to sound, clear and well-planned training. The average knowledge worker is quite capable of a week's course so long as the trainers make it relevant, and build a balance between content and process.
- Training courses of this nature must have a tangible outcome. It could be the award of a certificate signed by the trainers and the boss, for example. It might be a course dinner and photograph, and so on. The point is to make the delegates proud to have been on the course.
- Make sure that there is a sense of fun and adventure in the training. Training is enjoyable if done properly. And it is only memorable (i.e. people only learn anything) when they enjoy what they are doing.
- Introduce staff and work-force trainers to their change agents. Let them know that after the change training they are not going to be cut loose on their own for the rest of the change programme.

AN INDIVIDUAL 'TRAINING FOR CHANGE' SELF-NEEDS ASSESSMENT

We strongly recommend that prior to the installation of a training for change programme team leaders collate the following information about their staff. The following is a representative example of the type of form we use in establishing training needs when we are consulted as change consultants. (It should be borne in mind that, from the individual's point of view, the process of working through this form is often more useful than the answers produced by it.)

Change training needs assessment

Name _____   Number of people supervised _____

Dept _____   Time in position _____

Title _____   I report to _____

1. What do you think are the company's/department's top three goals, in order of importance?
2. What are the three most important objectives of your work area?
3. What are the three main obstacles you face in doing your job?
4. How would you describe the level of teamwork in the company/department? Why?
5. What does change mean to you?
6. Does your company/department currently have a climate that is receptive to change? Yes ☐ No ☐ Why?
7. Have you been on any change training courses? Yes ☐ No ☐ When?
8. If yes, describe the skills/concepts/areas that this/these course(s) covered.
9. What are the elements of your job that give you the most satisfaction?
10. What are your strengths as the leader of your team?
11. Using a 0–10 scale (0 = weak/5 = average/10 = excellent) please rate yourself first, and then any managers reporting to you, in the following areas (please do not personalise):

		Myself	Managers reporting to me
(a)	Receptiveness to change	_____	_____
(b)	Training for change	_____	_____
(c)	Communicating change	_____	_____
(d)	Empowering teams	_____	_____
(e)	Demonstrating openness	_____	_____
(f)	Motivating change	_____	_____
(g)	Delegating	_____	_____
(h)	Encouraging open challenge	_____	_____
(i)	Identifying driving and restraining forces to change	_____	_____
(j)	Identifying and unblocking resistance to change	_____	_____
(k)	Picking the right people for the new culture	_____	_____
(l)	Accepting new technologies	_____	_____
(m)	Setting clear objectives	_____	_____
(n)	Understanding the business we are in	_____	_____
(o)	Creating a supportive climate	_____	_____
(p)	Practising recognition	_____	_____
(q)	Encouraging quality management	_____	_____
(r)	Leading as opposed to governing	_____	_____
(s)	Having fun!	_____	_____

If you find yourself unable to answer many of the questions it reflects either your own lack of interest in the company or a lack of communication or team-awareness on the company's part. In other words, the organisation has not communicated its vision, goals etc. to its work-force. Low numerical answers to question 11 indicate areas where you might want to specifically discuss training needs with your training managers or personnel department.

Again, we stress that it is the process of working through the form that allows for the initial self-analysis prior to training needs discussions, rather than the specific results achieved.

11

THE CHANGE AGENTS

Although change is initiated from the top it has to be driven throughout the organisation. All management have the responsibility to make change happen, but successful change can only be brought about with some assistance. Most organisations have traditionally brought in outside consultants to assist in change programmes; and as consultants we have spent many years working on change projects worldwide.

It is from this experience of using consultants as facilitators that the concept of change agents has arisen. Organisational and change consultants, including those involved in cost-cutting and other efficiency drives, are best used in the planning stages of change programmes. They are also the experts necessary to deal with training for change where their experience of other organisations is invaluable. However, consultants should not be used in the direct implementation of change. That would mean that such changes would always be identified with the consultants or the consulting company. Management must be seen to take full charge of the change programme so that the staff and work-force accept that they, and their management, 'own' the new structure and procedures. Management must take credit for a successful change programme. The view of management must be 'We thought it up and we brought them in to help us in our project'.

Those in-house people who are responsible for the implementation of change are called the change agents, and although the role of the change agents will vary from organisation to organisation there is a general set of characteristics that we can look for in people who can become the champions of change in the organisation. Those characteristics must also be searched for by the change agents in others as they will have to, in turn, recruit subsequent change agents. By the end of the process every team, division and department will have an identifiable change agent who networks with all the others.

The role of the change agent is not to absolve management from the responsibility for making change happen; rather it is to become the expert in the process of change so that the staff and work-force know their point of contact in the change programme. This takes considerable time and effort, and it involves many consultations because, as this book demonstrates, the process cannot be imposed, and it requires the skills of balanced leadership.

One of the common challenges of staff faced with proposed change is to question the commitment of senior management to the programme. One role of the change agent is to demonstrate management's commitment; explaining what the organisation is doing to bring about the necessary change, and explaining the role taken by senior management in that change.

THE ROLES AND DUTIES OF THE CHANGE AGENTS

Before we examine the characteristics of change agents, let us look at their general role and duties they will perform in the change programme.

1. **To understand fully the reasons for the change programme** This understanding means that senior management must communicate to the change agents – in considerable detail – the overall plan and how it marries with the general strategy of the organisation. For many change agents recruited from the line and shop floor this is often the first time that

corporate strategy will have been communicated to them in this degree of detail. For that reason care must be taken not to frighten them off with unexplained, cold facts alone, which would give the impression of a brutal and uncaring change programme. Conversely, they should not end their briefing sessions thinking they can walk on water just because they are sharing privileged information about the organisation. The degree of openness in the organisation will normally determine the short-term effect of knowledge upon the change agent. Remember that the change agents themselves will have to communicate a greater part of the overall plan as part of the execution of their duties.

2. **To appreciate the risk of change** Moving an organisation from one position to another in terms of culture, technology, products and markets can often be a very high-risk move for the business. Senior management must share their concerns and fears, and they must share their calculations of risk and impact analysis. They should not forget to share their enthusiasm and optimism on a continuing basis. Risk must therefore be calculated, shared, monitored and updated throughout the change programme so that the change agents in turn can communicate this in the areas where they are working.

3. **To demonstrate their commitment to the changes through actions and verbal communication** If they exhibit any cynicism or hesitation about the change programme, this will be quickly exaggerated 'down the line'. Change agents must, however, avoid being evangelical as this will soon irritate the non-evangelists. Change agents must be professional, neutral and open in communicating what is happening and why it is happening.

4. **To appreciate the effect of change on people in the organisation as a whole and, in particular, the division or department that they are working in** Unless the individual change agents have lived through a series of change programmes themselves this will normally have to be done through training. Training is advisable anyway, since many change programmes

have faults and they are often remembered better, and are more exaggerated, than the successes. Even change agents of experience may need to be reminded of the good outcomes.

5. **To understand the impact the change process will have on the present culture of the organisation, and the impact on communication and reporting structures**

6. **To be aware of the impact, or possible impact, that the change will have upon the other parties affected, i.e. the customer, suppliers, local communities and so on**

7. **To establish what effect the change will have on the politics of the organisation, in particular the old traditional power blocks, the 'power relationships' which are found in any organisation** For example, traditionally powerful departments will fight tooth and nail if they perceive that the change is going to weaken their position in the organisation, even more so if they can identify who will be the new favoured departments or divisions.

8. **To seek out, record, recognise and, above all, make public the successes during the programme** This also means they must be ready to play down and laugh at failures as and when they arise, adhering to the principle that failure is only one of the building blocks of success.

9. **To earn and establish an independent stance in the change programme** The change agents must be neither management lackeys nor 'fronts' for the work-force.

10. **To communicate openly, on a regular basis, with fellow change agents to share experiences and act as communication channels between all sections of the organisation**

11. **To consult with both management and staff on necessary alterations to the change programme as they are identified**

12. **To assist in the training of management, staff and work-force in all the general aspects of the change programme** They must be poised to advise the training department in this regard

and authorised to commission outside help for specific technical and management training needs.

13. **Through leadership, they must communicate and encourage
    a sense of urgency, a sense of winning and a sense of fun in the
    change programme**

14. **To identify the ringleaders of resistance to the change pro-
    gramme, and to counsel and instruct them with a view to
    bringing them on board**   They should also identify those who
    cannot be 'won over'.

15. **To identify those people who are enthusiastic and energised
    by the change process and who may in turn become change
    agents themselves**

16. **To hold regular briefing meetings, and 'question and answer'
    sessions within departments and sections**   They must be
    ready to lead brainstorming and problem-solving meetings as a
    means of resolving resistance, conflicts, cynicism and lethargy
    to the change programme.

17. **To work closely with line management as part of the change
    team**

Other, more specific roles of the change agents will depend on the
size of the organisation, the nature of the change and the duration of
the change programme. Cultural change in an organisation may
mean a one-to-two-year process, but with change agents from each
department spending little more than, say, a couple of hours a week
on the process. On the other hand, the introduction of new plant
and working practices may mean the nomination of full-time
change agents. There can be no strict rules here, but change consultants can advise and offer guidelines from their experiences in
similar projects and from work in similar organisations. The following are examples of some of our outline recommendations on
change projects.

APPOINTMENT OF CHANGE AGENTS				
Nature of change	Change agents needed?	Full-time	Part-time	Number of agents
Cost-cutting	N	N/A	N/A	N/A
Cultural change	Y	N	Y	1 per 100
New technology	Y	Y	N	1 per 50
Reorganisation	Y	N	Y	1 per dept
Total quality	Y	Y	N	1 per dept
Relocation	Y	Y	N	1 per dept
Benchmarking	Y	Y	N	1 per 100

It is more difficult to establish the duration of the appointments; the only general rule is 'as long as it takes'.

WHAT MAKES A CHANGE AGENT?

We must now look at the general characteristics of what is needed in the change agent. Obviously, identifiable gaps can be supplemented by training, but in any mature organisation we would seek to identify – and would expect to find – people who demonstrate a high proportion of the following characteristics.

1. An identifiable and consistent management style that is in sympathy with the organisation.
2. Strong interpersonal skills: verbal communication skills; influencing skills; and effective presentation skills.
3. Knowledge of individual anchor points that help him or her cope with change, i.e. a knowledge of their own core values.
4. A knowledge of how to let go of the old situation in order to welcome the new situation, and a willingness to do so.
5. An ability to manage the anxieties and stresses that change will generate in people. Most of those will be unavoidably caused by

the change agent doing what needs to be done, allowing the change agent the advantage of managing such stresses as they are likely to arise.

6. The change agent must be willing and able to demonstrate overtly – through actions and highly visible behaviour – commitment to the change.

7. The agent must have an understanding of the organisational roles he or she prefers to occupy.

8. The agent must be capable of demanding, and securing, independence from the formal power blocks in the organisation.

9. The agent must have a strong allegiance to the company, its organisational aims and overall strategies. This is one key reason why the outside consultants cannot be the change agents; they may well be committed to the work, but their greatest advantage lies in being able to challenge the existing culture of the organisation in developing the change programme. External consultants who have challenged the company cannot then credibly exhibit strong allegiance to it (even though they may feel it).

10. Change agents must work in team situations. The agent must be a team player and must demonstrate leadership in team situations.

11. The agent must have curiosity and a sense of daring, and an inquisitive mind that does not seek the status quo.

12. The agent must have an understanding of his or her view of risk in a corporate sense, and must display the courage and tenacity to manage risk.

13. The agent must have a sense of adventure and fun which will energise and commit the teams.

14. The agent must be visionary, with the ability to view the overall project aims, and not get bogged down in trivia and detail.

15. The agent will need to be a good judge of character, and able and willing to delegate to others.

16. The agent must have, and use, networking skills both within and outside the company.

17. The agent must have a willingness to learn new ideas and remain flexible in attitude and behaviour.

18. The agent must be a lover of people rather than a lover of technology or systems. Change is a 'people' issue.

We can rarely expect to find all the characteristics we deem necessary for a successful change agent in single individuals. Few people can fulfil all the roles we have listed. A willingness on the part of the proposed change agent to learn and develop is the key to search for. With that, once weaknesses are identified, they can be addressed through training during the duration of the change project.

‖TRAINING CHANGE AGENTS

Training needs for change agents are continuous:

- pre-change training;
- training through the programme;
- post-change training.

The role of the change agent does not cease at the completion of the project. There is not only post-project work to be done, but the after-effects of change are usually long lived; it is better if the change agents are able to deal with them into the future. The change agent may have gone back to the line, or indeed a new job, but he or she should not cease to be a champion of change. Furthermore, their experience is invaluable for passing on to others for future change projects.

We recommend that the organisational training experts, usually the in-house training managers, conduct an in-depth needs assessment interview with the nominated change agents. In some organisations we have worked in we have been called in to assist at this stage as the training departments quite correctly realised that they had a lack of knowledge of the people and the core subjects involved. In most large companies, however, the training manager was part of the change agent selection process. We strongly recommend that any needs assessment discussion addresses the following issues.

1. Pre-change training

- Presentation skills, including presentation of statistic and financial information, assertiveness training where necessary.
- Leadership skills – this should be reinforcement training.
- Teambuilding.
- Chairing meetings.
- Recording techniques.

2. Training through the programme

- Problem-solving techniques.
- Motivation, reward and recognition.
- Training the trainers; in particular for learning styles.
- Risk analysis.
- Negotiating skills and counselling.

3. Post-change training

- Organisation development skills.
- The new culture of the organisation.
- Cost-cutting techniques.
- Total quality management.

Change agents need core, basic management skills to do the jobs which we have listed as pre-change training. During the change programme these skills need to be supplemented with practical training in order for them to run productive workshops, and communication exercises and meetings.

Lastly, we know that change is always with us and the close of one identifiable programme quickly leads to another. In order to capture what we have learnt from the change programme we must equip our change agents with other skills to analyse and record what happened.

In the largest organisations we have worked in, good change agents become what can only be described as professional change agents. They are recruited to do similar projects in other parts of the organisation, because of their skills. This is understandable, particularly in companies where there is almost always going to be some change programme under way. Often, after one or two years of dedication to the change project their original departments do not need them back. However, keeping such people full-time on change project work is denying the organisation a rich source of promotable management. In any case, even good change agents can become stale if left on project work too long.

One stint as a change agent should be seen as part of management development for all parts of the organisation and should not be seen as somewhere to put graduates in training. Nor should it be seen as a reward post for tired or near retiring senior managers.

CHANGE AGENTS IN SMALLER COMPANIES

The last point to make about change agents is how this role can be of benefit to small organisations who have to instigate change programmes. One management director of a small import–export company, with twelve employees, recently consulted us on this very issue. In order to meet international market expectations he had decided to instigate a BS5750 (quality) creditation through his small, young staff. Although he had never heard the expression 'change agent', he had correctly identified that there had to be a person, or persons, to push the programme through. It had to be someone that his staff could turn to. We were asked to undertake this role, but persuaded him that this was not a job for an external consultant. We took him through the roles and characteristics of change agents as we saw them in larger organisations.

Some time later, and after much soul searching, he came to the conclusion that he was the only person who could fulfil that particular role. We certainly could not disagree with him. In a small company, what better person to lead the change than the person most affected by it, the chief executive. The young staff were keen to get BS5750 but he, the owner, had the most difficult transition to go through.

Change agents are essential in both large and small organisations.

They can step outside the organisation and constraints, and evaluate what change means to the staff, work-force and the other stakeholders. They are both the champions and critics of the change process, but more importantly they are there to drive the change home and make it stick.

FOR POTENTIAL CHANGE AGENTS

The following questionnaire is designed to get potential change agents thinking about the behaviours they are going to use in implementing change in their chosen areas. It is also for change agents to use as a discussion and teaching document when encouraging individuals undergoing change programmes.

Rate your responses from 1 to 10 for each pair of statements.

I use standard approaches to problems								I approach problems in new ways	
1	2	3	4	5	6	7	8	9	10

I do not enjoy taking the initiative								I welcome the chance to take the initiative	
1	2	3	4	5	6	7	8	9	10

I do not easily accept new ideas								I am open to new ideas	
1	2	3	4	5	6	7	8	9	10

I feel comfortable in familiar ways of working								I am prepared to try new ways of doing things	
1	2	3	4	5	6	7	8	9	10

I try to agree with others								I try to challenge old ways and take an independent view	
1	2	3	4	5	6	7	8	9	10

I do not question the status quo								I challenge the status quo	
1	2	3	4	5	6	7	8	9	10

I prefer to stand back from important decisions								I stand firm on important issues	
1	2	3	4	5	6	7	8	9	10

I am afraid to turn my ideas into action								I turn ideas into action and get results	
1	2	3	4	5	6	7	8	9	10

If I think a thing will not work I say so								I find ways to make the unworkable work	
1	2	3	4	5	6	7	8	9	10

I act on problems as they arise								I anticipate problems before they arise	
1	2	3	4	5	6	7	8	9	10

I expect others to stick to my decisions								I try to understand the needs and desires of others	
1	2	3	4	5	6	7	8	9	10

I act according to what I think is right								I try to consider what others may think is right	
1	2	3	4	5	6	7	8	9	10

I expect to receive the respect and trust of others								I know I must build and earn the respect and trust of others	
1	2	3	4	5	6	7	8	9	10

I use the same style or approach, whatever the problem								I adapt my style and approach to suit the problem	
1	2	3	4	5	6	7	8	9	10

I expect people to work at work; their needs and feelings should be met at home

I encourage people to express their needs and feelings at work

| 1 | 2 | 3 | 4 | 5 | 6 | 7 | 8 | 9 | 10 |

People must find ways to motivate themselves

My actions and behaviour should motivate others

| 1 | 2 | 3 | 4 | 5 | 6 | 7 | 8 | 9 | 10 |

I take what responsibility I have to take

I am always seeking new responsibilities

| 1 | 2 | 3 | 4 | 5 | 6 | 7 | 8 | 9 | 10 |

I defer problems to a later time

I meet problems head on

| 1 | 2 | 3 | 4 | 5 | 6 | 7 | 8 | 9 | 10 |

I leave problems to others

I enjoy solving problems

| 1 | 2 | 3 | 4 | 5 | 6 | 7 | 8 | 9 | 10 |

I blame others if things do not go right

I accept responsibility if things do not go right

| 1 | 2 | 3 | 4 | 5 | 6 | 7 | 8 | 9 | 10 |

I am afraid of failure

I see failure as a stepping-stone to success

| 1 | 2 | 3 | 4 | 5 | 6 | 7 | 8 | 9 | 10 |

I avoid taking risks

I take calculated risks

| 1 | 2 | 3 | 4 | 5 | 6 | 7 | 8 | 9 | 10 |

People must learn by their mistakes

I give time and effort towards coaching others

| 1 | 2 | 3 | 4 | 5 | 6 | 7 | 8 | 9 | 10 |

People need to be told when they are falling down on the job

I encourage others to monitor their own progress

| 1 | 2 | 3 | 4 | 5 | 6 | 7 | 8 | 9 | 10 |

I do not give praise or criticism								I give praise and constructive feedback whenever needed	
1	2	3	4	5	6	7	8	9	10

My team is never certain of its objectives								My team discusses and sets its objectives clearly	
1	2	3	4	5	6	7	8	9	10

I like to solve problems in my own way, and then tell others what I have done								I like to work with others towards a joint solution	
1	2	3	4	5	6	7	8	9	10

Team communications are bad								Team communications are good	
1	2	3	4	5	6	7	8	9	10

I withhold praise and recognition								I give praise and recognition	
1	2	3	4	5	6	7	8	9	10

I seek out the weaknesses of others and manipulate them								I seek out the strengths of others and encourage them	
1	2	3	4	5	6	7	8	9	10

I deal with people according to my needs								I deal with people according to their needs	
1	2	3	4	5	6	7	8	9	10

I do not feel the need to gain the commitment of others								I like to get the commitment of others	
1	2	3	4	5	6	7	8	9	10

I only ask people to do what I know they are capable of								I offer people challenges to stretch them, and give support where they need it	
1	2	3	4	5	6	7	8	9	10

I give people a job and tell them how to do it							I let others 'own' their job		
1	2	3	4	5	6	7	8	9	10

I like to work in isolation							I like to work with others		
1	2	3	4	5	6	7	8	9	10

I do not have good, participative working relationships with others							I create strong working relationships with others		
1	2	3	4	5	6	7	8	9	10

The 'politics' of the work-place do not concern me							I am aware of the 'politics' of the work-place		
1	2	3	4	5	6	7	8	9	10

I keep information to myself and use it to my advantage							I pool knowledge to improve the overall effectiveness of the work		
1	2	3	4	5	6	7	8	9	10

I expect others to work out the benefits of tasks							I explain my understanding of the benefits of tasks, and seek the opinions of others		
1	2	3	4	5	6	7	8	9	10

I blame people for failure and punish them							I praise success and look for ways to build on failure		
1	2	3	4	5	6	7	8	9	10

Evaluation

The reader will readily recognise that the higher the total score the more open to change the individual must be.

Below 100: indicates an irrational and unreasonable resistance to change.

100–200: too rigid thinking; the issues discussed in this book need to be carefully addressed.

200–300:   you have joined the majority of people who are taking a serious attitude to change and have the potential to be successful change managers.

300–399:   you are a natural change leader and should lead change at every possible opportunity

400   You lack imagination even when cheating!

12 | IMPLEMENTING CHANGE

Before we can implement the change programme the following must be in place and agreed.

- The agreed programme for change, as set out in Chapter 9.
- The appointment of trained change agents, as discussed in Chapter 11.
- Those involved should have been informed and consulted about the change process. Prior to implementation, management must have communicated the implementation programme to all levels of the organisation. The responsibility for making change happen lies with all management, staff and work-force representatives who, at this stage, must take ownership of the change programme.
- Those who cannot agree with the change programme must be identified and counselled. Obviously, in time, those who most strongly oppose the change will seek to leave, or may be encouraged to leave, the organisation. The least we will demand of those who wish to remain in the organisation is that they do not block the change process in the areas that they implement. Hopefully, when the successes start to become visible and are communicated through the organisation, these people will eventually see the sense and necessity of the change programme.

Up to this point the programme has still been largely on the drawing board. It is now, at the implementation stage, that the natural resistances to change and the blocking mechanisms of the organisational power blocks will come into play.

The implementation programme we recommend to management is the following ten-point plan:

1. agree the time frame;
2. agree the overall goals;
3. agree the strategy;
4. agree the interventions to be used;
5. watch, observe and record the change process;
6. evaluate the findings;
7. take corrective action;
8. identify the blocks to change;
9. capture the leaders of resistance;
10. publish the success.

We will now look at these points in detail.

1. Agree the time frame

The change implementation programme must have a definite start point and a clearly defined finish. Change is disturbing for most people, but can be accepted more readily when they know what is going to happen and when it will be over. As with all emotional shifts the quicker the programme the better. For this reason it is essential to break the programme into manageable, 'stand-alone', pieces of work. For instance, if the organisation is being restructured there is no reason why each department cannot be treated as a mini project. This may be better than starting restructuring in secret and keeping everyone in suspense until all the departmental changes have been fed up the line; and then, on some magic day, publishing the results. In our experience change programmes usually take far longer than is really necessary to implement. This is normally due to cowardly managers who are afraid to take risks. They implement a bit of the programme, then stand back to see the effect before taking the next plunge.

Consultants – outside contractors – cannot implement the

change programme, although they would be likely to be the ones who are bravest enough to do it properly. Consultants should be used in planning and training for change; they will have considerable experience from earlier change projects in other organisations. However, the programme is the line management's responsibility and must not be delegated to third parties. The programme must always be seen as being owned by management, not consultants. There must never be an excuse to blame others if the implementation does not work. In any case, although consultants may be capable of implementing change programmes they could procrastinate, delaying the implementation for various and obvious reasons; they cease to be paid when the job is done.

The more difficult issue is the question of how long the implementation programme should take. Again, on this the advice and experience of outside change experts are invaluable. The time plan is not really scientifically calculable, but working on previous projects does give a 'feel' as to the number of days necessary. As an example, if we were restructuring a department of fifty people the mini project could look like this:

50 interviews with members of staff at 2 hours per session	20 days
Evaluation of findings	3 days
Drafting out the new structure	2 days
Consultation with departmental heads	5 days
Submission of plan to management	1 day
Agreement of plan (i.e. obtaining permissions from unions, health and safety, auditors etc.)	5 days
Briefing all staff and publication of new structure	14 days
Contingency and fine-tuning allowances	14 days

This gives a total operational time of around thirteen weeks. From our experience when restructuring a department we would allow some additional time for briefings, depending on the likely strength of staff resistance.

Obviously this time plan is implemented within the change programme, i.e. within clearly defined goals. Although the time plan may sometimes prove to be unreliable, it is a motivational goal to aim at and should not be relaxed except in extreme circumstances. In such a case the reasons for the delays should be made public.

2. Agree the overall goals

Any implementation programme must have a clear result, i.e. the goals must be agreed in advance and made public throughout the organisation. It may seem obvious, but from our experience management needs to be reminded that the change project is not successful if the company comes through it just looking different; it has to be the difference that was planned for or it has not been a success. Senior management goals may have quite a high level of abstraction, for example: 'reduce costs by 20 per cent'. However, the subsidiary objectives have to be drawn up in much more detail for the divisions and departments to tackle. It is essential that, as always, department heads are brought in at this point, made part of the implementation process and fully empowered to make management decisions within the programme. Although the board may have set the goal of a 20 per cent reduction in costs, it must be up to the departmental heads to recommend how and where the savings may be made. This will give them a sense of ownership of the project and, more importantly, a sense of control. In the natural defence of their employees, management will often offer ingenious methods of savings within their areas, rather than sacrifice their staff.

Let us now look more closely at the goals of a change project using relocation (one of the commonest changes companies have to go through) as an example. The basis of the assumption is that the board and senior management of the company have decided to relocate from London to Cardiff in order to save office, staff and administration costs. They have determined that the whole project should be completed within twelve months. The overall goals from their point of view, and as stated by them, may look like this:

1. to relocate from London to Cardiff within twelve months;
2. to identify new office accommodation within quarter 1; ·
3. to identify which management staff will be offered relocation to Cardiff and those who are to be made redundant within quarter 2;

4. to have available human resource plans on staff organisation and costs of moving staff, including relocation expenses by end of quarter 2;

5. to receive departmental plans by the end of quarter 2 relating to customers, suppliers etc.;

6. to start recruiting and training local staff in Cardiff by quarter 3;

7. to fit and equip new offices within quarter 3;

8. to move pilot management and staff in during quarter 3;

9. to commence closure of old office etc. in quarter 3;

10. to identify and locate support functions, i.e. accountants, lawyers, bankers etc. in quarter 3.

It will be obvious from the above that each goal is clearly defined and would have an outline time implementation plan. This would be fed to the implementation team who will then calculate the critical path.

The goals should be achievable and understood by all. The total plan should be made public so that every member of the staff and work-force understands where they fit in and what is expected from them within the time frame. The communication should be in straightforward language, and may be assisted by diagrams and charts explaining why the goals must be met in certain times in order to keep the project on its critical path.

3. Agree the strategy

Up to this point we now know what we want to do and by when we want to do it. The strategy of implementation now asks the question of how we are going to do it. There are various matters of detail to be considered.

- Is the implementation plan going to be a top-down or bottom-up process, or a mixture of both?
- How do we consult with individuals, teams, departments etc.?
- What will we offer our staff, and by when do we need to know their responses?
- Will the change be made division by division, department by department or will there be what is graphically known as a napalm approach (go for the lot in one go!)?

- What degree of empowerment are we going to allow departmental managers in the decisions to be made?
- Which methods of communication are we going to use to inform our staff of what is happening?
- What external assistance are we going to use, and when?
- What training strategies are we going to use?
- What benchmarks are we going to use to compare the effects of change, i.e. how do we measure success?
- What is it going to cost us and who is going to monitor the budget?

4. Agree the interventions to be used

In order to implement change we must use some forms of interventions to coach, motivate and drive the change home. The use of interventions can be both crude and subtle, but they must be understood by everybody and they must not be thought of as being manipulative. For instance, if we are closing down a plant over a period of time then there will come a point in the project where some people will still have to operate the plant, knowing that in a few months' time they will be made redundant. In this case it may be necessary to offer loyalty bonuses to keep production running smoothly. The rule of interventions is that they must be used sparingly and they must not become a 'right'; if they become 'normal' they lose their effect. Keeping interventions in place over a period of time can often wear people out where they are performing over and above normal expectations. We must also remember that learning overload is possible where we are cramming too much information into people within a very short time frame. Examples of some of the common interventions used on change projects are as follows:

- training;
- loyalty bonuses;
- relocation expenses;
- time off in lieu;
- group team bonuses;
- recognition parties;
- increase of status;

- incentives, i.e. company cars, shareholdings etc.;
- increased promotion prospects.

5. Watch, observe and record the change process

Change often becomes a very personal issue. Here, the role of the change agents is most important; their job is to help the transition of change. 'New working methods' is an example of a change where people often feel most uncomfortable. If a person has been doing a successful job for the last, say, ten years and then finds in a change programme that he or she has to work in a different way the effect of change can be quite brutal upon that individual. Questions arise in his or her mind such as, 'What have I been doing wrong all these years?' and 'Do I like working in the new way?'

All people will work within a new method for a time, but without some follow-up and reinforcement they will readily slip back to their old method of working. At the very least they will tend to refine the new method to suit themselves. This may turn out to be a good thing in the long run, but in the early days of change the new methods must be operated according to the plan. This will let the planners see what effect their plan has had upon the overall working of the department or division, and ultimately the organisation.

It is therefore necessary for the change agents, and front-line management, to watch what is happening, observe the new method in practice and record the effect, and by asking staff and the work-force to record the effects of the changes themselves. Over a short period of time empowered middle management can relax the rules and allow refinements of the new methods to be put into place, but these refinements must also be observed and recorded.

Obviously, one of the advantages of empowering our people to refine the new methods is to make them feel part of the change process. Another is to let them appreciate that they are in control of their new work processes.

In our experience one of the basic reasons for failure of change initiatives is the obstinacy of consultants and managements in not allowing refinements to the new working methods. This is often because the change plan has become their baby (their ownership), and they forget the overall purpose of the plan and its effects on the client's staff. Where possible we recommend that the work teams themselves observe and record the change process: the change agents can be used as co-ordinators for this.

6. Evaluate the findings

At some stage in the change process it is necessary to evaluate the findings, i.e. find out what we have done and what effect this is having upon the organisation and the business. It cannot be stated too strongly that necessary change is evolutionary, and should be welcomed and encouraged, but the business must still function. The effect of change upon the management, staff and work-force, as well as other stakeholders, must be evaluated and considered. We recommend the following courses of action.

- The effect of change upon the management can be analysed in brainstorming sessions. It is wise to use an outside facilitator who is skilled in this task.
- The effect on the staff can be monitored by staff surveys and 'bitching sessions'. Bitching sessions are defined as times when a member of staff is allowed, without interruption and in complete confidence, and with no come-back, to speak for, say, five minutes, and air his or her fears and worries about what is going on in the company.
- The effect upon the work-force should be monitored through surveys, questionnaires, group discussions with management and work-force representatives.
- The effect on customers can be monitored through customer visits and seminars.
- The effect on the local community can be monitored through surveys and local meetings, site visits and so on.
- The effect on suppliers can be monitored through visits of suppliers to the organisation, and by visiting the suppliers themselves.
- There are a number of telephone surveys that may be useful; examining the effect upon the City, institutions, bankers etc.
- Discussion groups and invitations to analysts to come and visit the organisation post-change may provide useful feedback.

The size and nature of the organisation will determine what is expedient and how it is done. It must be remembered that change is like dropping a pebble into a pond; there is always a 'ripple effect'. It is dangerous, in the long run, to ignore the effect of change upon all parts of the business, both internal and external.

7. Take corrective action

From the feedback arising from the above it will always be necessary to take corrective action. Such action should be immediate and effective. Corrective action must be made visible to those affected, and there should always be explanations of why it was necessary. If necessary reinstitute the previous working methods and rethink the whole process rather than struggle with something that looked good at the planning stage, but at the moment is not doing the job. With major change it may be necessary to blitz the problem and throw new resources at it. This is particularly true of sensitive areas, i.e. in the customer environments and the financial institutions.

The feedback from the above should be given to corrective action teams (CAT teams) made up of those people doing the job where the problems are arising, and led by the resident change agent. There may be brainstorming sessions and workshops needed to determine the course of the corrective action. Experts, including the representatives of manufacturers, suppliers, customers, local community etc. should be involved and made part of the problem-solving process. Timing is important and speed is of the essence. When corrective action has been taken it may be necessary to rework the evaluation of findings to see what effect it has had.

A word of warning though: do not get panicked into taking corrective action too quickly. Staff and the work-force are experts at exaggerating problems, and masters of the art of panicking management into fire-fighting mode.

8. Identify the blocks to change

The next stage in the implementation programme is to identify the blocks to change. In any organisation of size there will be power blocs who will often resist change. In 1984, Professor Child

published his contingency theory where he recognised that organisations are structured not only for task, i.e. doing the job, but for
political reasons as well. He argued that the organisation structure
is not simply a function of making things as efficient as possible, but
is often also a function of what is acceptable to various power
blocs and management groups within the organisation. The distribution of such power may vary from time to time; different groups
may manoeuvre themselves into positions of influence or resist
change in the organisational structure. It is argued then that in some
organisations efficiency is not the prime reason for existence; the
main driving function being the power relationships. If this is so
then any attempt to change the organisation will be met with
resistance.

For example, on recent change work we were met with a so-called
internal mafia. These were perceived power blocs that we tackled
at our peril. The only common factor, which works to the change
planners' advantage, is that normally the power blocs are known,
stable and identifiable. As consultants we were able to communicate with them openly, and face their issues. If resistance to
change by an individual is natural, as we have argued in this book,
then resistance to change by a comfortable power bloc is even
more natural. Our job as consultants in this case – with the aid of the
change agents – was to talk to this group to understand what they
were defending. In most cases, as in this one, it became obvious that
they were defending privilege; the exercise of power interventions
was used to get them on board. Obviously relocation or spreading
them around would have been pointless; the power bloc is
normally drawn from different departments in any case. Remember
when dealing with such power blocs that they are defending the
status quo as they have been taught and encouraged to do in the
past. Apart from the power blocs other blocks to change must be
identified.

The most common blocks, real and perceived, are as follows:

- lack of commitment from senior management;
- middle management (often referred to as the marzipan layer);
- lack of empowerment – everybody waiting for somebody else to
  take decisions and make things happen;

- out-of-date working methods and systems or out-of-date technology that cannot operate the new methods;
- inappropriate organisation structures;
- the organisation being strangle-held by a dominant department, i.e. engineering or accounts;
- the management style;
- an organisation that has lost faith in itself;
- cynical and tired senior management;
- untrained work-force;
- overworked and tired front-line management;
- an organisation no longer in control of itself, or one being run by a financial institution;
- an organisation being run on reputation alone.

9. Capture of the leaders of resistance

The penultimate stage of the implementation programme is to capture the leaders of resistance to change. While we have argued that management must be tolerant of the natural resistance to change, in any change programme there will come a point when any more resistance is counter-productive and cannot be tolerated. To go beyond that point would undermine the change and defeat the whole purpose of the exercise. When people think they are defending the status quo with a good leader they will enjoy resisting management and the organisation in the change process.

Carping or ridiculing success, and constantly reinforcing the historical viewpoint, is a safe and comfortable pastime for these people. What, then, can management and the change agents do?

Our preferred method is to make such people change agents themselves. This makes them not only defend the change process, but become part of the planning and implementation of it. From our experience most sound, professional people will accept the challenge of being a poacher turned gamekeeper. In some of the projects we have been involved with it is ironic that the restrainers to change often become its strongest allies as they learn more about the change process.

Unfortunately, there will always be the few that, because of their position in the organisation, feel they have nothing to lose. Or they may believe that their own power base in the company will resist the change. These people are often experts in some specialist field, or those nearing retirement. These people must be sought out and removed with the same surgical precision that the police use when quelling riots; identify the ringleaders and get them out of the way quickly. Our advice is to neuter them by the simple expediency of either early retirement or voluntary redundancy. In other words, and to extend the mafia analogy used earlier, 'make them an offer they can't refuse'. If a person has such a special and peculiar skill that they are indeed invaluable, then they can always be employed as consultants until arrangements can be made for a transfer of skills and knowledge. Once they become consultants their influence as leaders in a resistance movement is normally broken.

10. Publish the success

Lastly, but most importantly, publish the successes. Human nature cannot resist success. Any change programme will have numerous successes, and these must be made as public and visible as possible. As the whole organisation is made aware of success people will feel more confident and want to join in.

Publishing success can take many forms, depending on the culture of the organisation. In organisations we have worked with we have seen dedicated newsletters, video films, boasting sessions, group meetings, articles in company magazines, as well as the more traditional routes of notice boards and communication down the line. What types of things should be published will depend upon the nature of change being implemented, but here are a few examples:

- meeting a key date ahead of, or on, the time plan;
- implementing a change within budget;
- the establishment of a successful new working method;
- achieving cost savings;
- receiving customer praise;
- good press reports;
- favourable City comment;
- reaching agreement with representatives of the staff and the work-force;

- increase in production;
- increase in profit or decrease in losses;
- successful disposal of assets;
- innovative mergers and alliances;
- sales figures;
- increase in customer base;
- new product launch;
- successful introduction of new technology;
- reduction of lost time accidents;
- reduction in overtime, but throughput constant;
- corrective action team results;
- value-for-money improvements with suppliers.

Our golden rule is simple; if in doubt, publish it.

The reader will readily see that the potential list is endless. But the problem with success is that we often forget that it is part of the process and it is important in ensuring continuing confidence in the long-term change project, or for the next project. Rashly, it is often left to nothing more reliable than word of mouth.

A commonly seen example of broad public 'boasting' is adopted by building companies working on motorway and other roadworks where, when applicable, they put up large signs after the job is done stating for instance 'Bypass completed six months ahead of schedule. XYZ Ltd seen to be serving the community', or whatever.

Another recent example is British Rail's television publicity to show that it is making an often successful effort to reduce the lateness of trains on certain lines.

Our advice is make it public and do it in the company's equivalent of flashing neon lights!

(The setting out of plans for more complex change programmes can often be aided with the use of diagrams. These may also be an easier way of communicating complex plans to others. We suggest that the reader faced with complex planning should turn to Chapter 15 to see the two most useful forms of diagram available as tools of such planning and communication.)

13 | OUTSOURCING: A PATTERN FOR THE FUTURE

Patterns are emerging in our industries of what future business organisations may look like. It should be stressed that from experience it appears such patterns are cyclical; the next stage will give way to different patterns in the more distant future. No doubt some of the ideas regarded as outdated now will have their day again some time.

However, the most immediate change that seems to be happening, and seems to have a reasonably long 'shelf-life', is that of outsourcing.

A TRADITIONAL WAY OF OPERATING

Outsourcing has always been a way of getting work done when the company did not have, or did not seek to employ, the people with the skills to do it. In other words, companies have often brought in consultants, or given contracts out to subcontractors.

Small companies have always done it, of course. A two-partner firm of decorators will have all the decorating skills it needs, but it will outsource everything else; accounts to the accountant and typing to the spouse, for example.

That trend continues of course, but it has been dramatically extended of late. For the first time we are seeing outsourcing not so much as a way of 'filling the skills gaps', but as a way of getting back to core business.

Companies over the past decades have engaged in horizontal and vertical integration. Horizontal integration is the buying up of, or merging with, your competitors. Vertical integration is the buying up of the chain of production; for example, retailers might buy warehouses and become wholesalers, and might reach back as far as manufacturing, and even to raw material extraction. This has meant that organisations have drawn away from their former main business.

Certain work has often been subcontracted, even with integrated companies; for example on-site security is usually left to external security companies. Advertising is also an example of an activity that is outsourced because it is a specialist function that is called for only when needed.

However, it has been recognised that companies do not always operate well when they are outside their core business. Even though the integration may have taken the form of buying existing companies skilled in their own areas, the intrusion of the new 'holding company' has often made those companies less effective than they once were. In times of recession, particularly, companies have recognised that their greatest contribution to profits is usually coming from the core business, perhaps one for which they are traditionally known. Financial analysis of results achieved has often indicated that in fact the core business had been subsidising losses in the other companies.

SELLING OFF DEPARTMENTS

More recently, companies have sold off their integrations and allowed the companies to sink or swim on their own. Often they have been given contracts to continue operating with the main company.

The principle of subcontracting has now been extended from this, however. Companies are 'selling off' their own departments on the same basis. One major oil and exploration company has recently outsourced its entire accounts department to a firm of specialist consultants. The logic is that the company can concentrate totally on oil and exploration, and have a team of managers running outsourced 'departments'. The move has therefore been from out-sourcing specialist functions that are rarely needed, to outsourcing everyday functions in constant use (but which are non-core activities).

Advantages of outsourcing

- The company concentrates on what it is good at, and does not divert attention to areas where it is 'reinventing wheels' that others have already invented.
- It removes bureaucracy from the company.
- It cuts costs, replacing staff and associated overheads with fixed price contracts. This means that the outsourcee companies have to do the calculations necessary to keep within the quoted prices.
- Outsourcees look after themselves. The company giving out the contracts (the outsourcer) does not have responsibility for training, personnel problems, absenteeism and so on.

Disadvantages of outsourcing

- Companies do not train staff they are not employing. This forces the training function to be dealt with by the outsourcee com-panies. However, the company giving out the contracts no longer has control over the quality of the training. It is thought that this could become a problem in time if the right skills are not being trained. We are already hearing complaints such as 'apprentices learn the tricks of the trade, without first learning the trade'. However, we are already seeing the outsourcee companies buy-ing training services from the outsourcers; outsourcee staff are now sitting on training courses run 'in-house' by the outsourcers.
- Some companies will have to train even subcontractors in their individual health and safety needs. The skills may, to some

extent, be transferable, with the result that a lot of the training budget may be used where there will be no return. In one client company they had outsourced all the scaffolding erection work that they had formerly done in-house. The scaffolding company that took the contract had been used to 'standard' building work, but not to the specialist needs of a complex, industrial process plant. A huge scaffolding column holding over forty people collapsed as a result of the contractors' lack of the right experience (fortunately there were no serious injuries on that occasion).

- Outsourcees could become a monopoly (the only source of supply) and that could result in higher prices, and the loss of the cost-cutting advantage first sought.
- Outsourcee companies could face a situation where their contract is with a monopsony (the only source of demand). If that company closes down, changes its core business or seeks other contracts, then the outsourcee may have no buyer for its services.
- Outsourcees create a subculture within the company. This subculture is not part of the company, just living within it in symbiosis. Subcontractors do not 'play the company games', do not get involved socially with the full-time work-force and have no sense of commitment to the company, management or employees.
- Outsourcees can become a focus of envy for the full-time employees. They often earn a lot of money and have easy access to 'overtime'. The fact that they do not get holiday pay, company perks and so on is not so visible.

Whether or not outsourcing will prove to be a long-term proposal, or a quick fix, is yet to be seen. Certainly some managers are enjoying the situation it creates. They become a department of one, with full managerial salary and perks, but have no staff. The old joke of companies was often 'this department would work better if there were no staff to worry about'. Suddenly that joke is coming true.

IF YOU BECOME AN OUTSOURCEE

Individuals are often finding that they are being made redundant by their companies and then taken back as subcontractors. There are a few hurdles with the Inland Revenue to jump over on this, but they do not concern us here. What must be set out are the principal areas that you might have to consider if you find yourself in this position.

- You will not be part of the company pension scheme. You will need to contribute to a pension scheme of your own. This can be arranged through independent advisers. Advice on this subject will be available from banks, accountants and solicitors.
- You will almost certainly need the services of an accountant to help you understand the rules relating to self-employment, and to advise on keeping appropriate records to satisfy legal requirements.
- You will be responsible for your own taxation and national insurance payments. You will need to budget for these payments as you will no longer have tax deducted 'weekly' or 'monthly', as under the PAYE system. Your accountant will advise on these matters.
- You may need to register for VAT and keep appropriate records to satisfy the VAT office. Again, your accountant will be able to advise on this.
- You will have to negotiate contracts. This is a skill in its own right and you may be advised to seek training in this regard. You will almost certainly need to use a solicitor to advise on the construction of such contracts.
- You will need personal time-management skills. There is a huge difference between being self-employed and being employed. You will earn only what you work for, and not just for 'being at your desk'. You will face competition from others who want your contracts and you will need to be efficient to prevent them 'undercutting' you in bidding.
- You will need to maintain your own training in your professional and technical skills to avoid falling behind the competition you

have suddenly acquired. This is a cost and time constraint that you must budget for. You will be expected to keep up to date with the latest technologies in your field.

- You will need your own equipment for the most part. At its most basic you will need a car. Subcontractors are rarely given company cars, particularly as this can cause difficult tax problems with the Inland Revenue.
- You will need to practise networking skills. You may be called on to introduce skills that are not yours in order to complete a contract.
- You must keep up your contacts; part of networking. As one contract is ending, you must be poised to tender for another.

OUTSOURCED DEPARTMENTS AND FUNCTIONS

In the companies we have been working with, the following departments and functions have been outsourced:

- accountancy;
- advertising;
- building services;
- canteen;
- cleaning;
- distribution and warehousing;
- information technology services;
- medical services;
- office moving;
- personnel functions;
- planned and programmed maintenance (plant shut-downs etc.);
- salaries and wages;
- secretarial services;
- security;
- share registration;
- training;
- travel services;
- vehicle fleet maintenance.

As the trend continues we are left wondering what the future definition of 'core activities' is likely to be. It is not impossible to imagine a major corporation consisting of nothing but managers of a totally outsourced business.

III

TOOLS FOR CHANGE

14 | SPECIFIC INDICATORS OF THE NEED FOR CHANGE

As much as we believe that there are few companies that would not benefit from change programmes or culture change in some form or the other, it is equally true that some companies adopt change programmes because 'it is the in thing to do'. Of course, many of those companies need change programmes; unfortunately they often pick the wrong ones.

There can be many and complex reasons why companies need to change; but in this chapter we examine some of the more obvious pointers that can be found easily by asking the question, 'Does my company need to change?'

These indicators are more directed at strategic changes than cultural ones; however, most companies that need strategic change usually find that the need arises on the back of a changing culture.

▌IF MONEY IS THE MEASURE. . .

The most obvious indicators of a need for change can be found in the accounts where there is an agreed measure that can be compared to other years, or other companies.

It would be naïve to suggest that companies exist only to make money and generate profits. As this book has shown modern companies have acknowledged that people spending so much of their waking life working need their companies to fulfil other requirements in their lifestyles. However, it would also be naïve to believe that companies can exist without making money and profits. Profits are the self-generated income of the company: they provide the resources for expansion and the reward for shareholders in the form of dividend payments. Companies can survive making losses in the short term if they can live off their previously generated profits or make short-term borrowings, but in the long term companies must make profits overall to be viable. For this reason the flow of money and profits in the company is a very good indication of the health and direction of the company.

None of the indicators in this chapter should be taken alone as there can often be very good reasons for apparently adverse financial positions. It is the cumulative effect of these, and other, areas of information that indicate the need for strategic change. Furthermore, none of the solutions offered are necessarily always right for all situations. In some cases what will help one company will harm another. These are illustrative only; the final changes being decided on after full and complex analysis.

SOURCES AND APPLICATION OF CAPITAL

The various types of capital in a company are its 'piggy banks'. There are various piggy banks for various purposes. First, there are the 'permanent' sources of capital: money invested by the shareholders when they buy shares in the company, and also the company's own generated profits. All of these are permanent in the sense that, with rare exceptions, they are never repayable. In addition to the permanent capital are the long-term sources of finance: long-term loans and fixed-interest debenture borrowings.

The 'piggy banks' holding permanent and long-term capital should only be broken into to buy assets of equally long life. For example, if you were buying a piece of machinery that you knew would last ten years then it would be reasonable to borrow the money to buy it over a ten-year period.

Companies in financial difficulties will borrow from whatever source is possible to maintain their position. Invariably, financial difficulties cause the company to focus on the short-term view, but directors will often begin to authorise long-term borrowings to finance the short-term position. An analysis of the balance sheet examining the values of long-term assets owned by the company against which there are long-term borrowings – and particularly a time series analysis over the past, say, five years – is likely to give some indication of a struggling company in need of a strategic change.

Of course, companies need to survive in the short term if they are to survive in the long term. Short-term solutions may be needed. However, a strategy for the long-term must correct the problems that short-term (quick fix) solutions are dealing with. In the above situation a company might consider selling some of its fixed assets and leasing them back. 'Sale and lease back' is a common practice. It produces a sum of money that can be used to pay off long-term debts and perhaps provide a working capital injection for immediate trading needs. The lease payments may then easily be met out of trading in the new, healthier company.

There are one or two specialist sources of finance which often indicate that a company may be having cash-flow difficulties and therefore require strategic change in its policies.

Factoring and invoice discounting

Although these two types of short-term financing are quite different, they basically amount to getting someone else to deal with your debt collection while improving your cash flow. The factoring or discounting company pays you more quickly for your outstanding debts than your debtors would. These methods of improving cash flow are, generally speaking, expensive and tend to be used by companies as a last resort. They usually indicate that the company is in short-term cash-flow difficulty and that traditional sources of lending, such as the banks, have refused assistance. An examination of the company showing a move towards this type of financing may indicate that it requires strategic change planning. Such planning may include searching for more reliable customers, educating the sales force to consider the collection of debts when closing a sale (sales reps often see their job done when the contract is signed and give little thought to after-sales cash collection), or training inside the credit control department to ensure that they are up to date on all the ways to collect debts from resistant customers.

(It should be noted that there are certain types of industries, jewellery retail is probably the most obvious, where these types of financing are considered normal and would not therefore give rise to concern unless there were other indications as well.)

	APW (Holdings) plc		
	Movement of assets and liabilities		
	over a 2-year period		
	Balance Sheet 1991	Balance Sheet 1992	Movement (taken as + or − asset position)
FIXED ASSETS			
Freehold buildings	40,000	80,000	40,000 (+ asset)
Plant/equipment	20,000	50,000	30,000 (+ asset)
CURRENT ASSETS AND LIABILITIES			
Stock	15,000	40,000	25,000 (+ asset)
Debtors	–	20,000	20,000 (+ asset)
Cash	25,000	(10,000)	35,000 (− asset)
Creditors	(25,000)	(40,000)	15,000 (− asset)
	£75,000	£140,000	£65,000
Represented by:			
Share capital	75,000	75,000	–
Retained profit	–	65,000	65,000
	£75,000	£140,000	£65,000
			('Flow of funds')

PROFITABILITY AND THE USE OF THE PROFITS

If a company is continually making losses there will be an obvious concern for its survivability in the long term. However, the fact that a company is making profits does not mean that its financial strategy is necessarily correct. Cash flow, and the document in the accounts called the 'Statement of source and application of funds', show the management's application of profits being made. Those applications will say much about the financial acumen of the management and, if there are adverse signs, will indicate the need for change.

This is best demonstrated by way of a simple example. Consider the compared balance sheets shown opposite.

The company has increased its net value by £65,000. This suggests that there has been some good management at least at some level. However, the creation of wealth is not reflected in the bank. The bank balance has gone down from a positive balance of £25,000 to a negative position, an overdraft, of £10,000; a deterioration of £35,000. This alone does not have to be a bad thing, as too much liquidity would be a waste of resources. The question is, however, what has been done with the profit and the cash? The answer is that with the £65,000 profit and the deterioration of £35,000 cash position, a total of £100,000 has been applied in the following way:

£70,000 has been invested in long-term assets
£25,000 has been invested in stocks (possibly unwisely)
£20,000 has effectively been loaned to our customers by not asking
         them to pay their debts (the increase in debtors)
                                                        _____
                                                        £115,000

In order to bridge the gap between the £100,000 and the £115,000 creditors have increased by £15,000, i.e. we have had to take money from our suppliers by not paying them, which may antagonise them in the short term.

The position is that the company has adopted a programme of long-term investment which may be useless if it cannot survive in

the short term. The immediate indications of this shift in the balance
sheet is that it would not survive long in the short term on this
current strategy. The company has not recognised that a large
portion of its profit must be reinvested into the working capital, i.e.
the short-term monies available for day-to-day living. The company
may not now be able to pay for the goods and services it needs, or
pay its wages, to keep in business. In periods of recession such
companies are vulnerable and die off very quickly, since they have
no fat through which to survive lean periods.

This sort of time series analysis of balance sheets indicates a great
deal about management's ability to plan strategically and indicates
where the need for strategic change in a company may be urgent.

In the example above, it might be prudent to consider less purchasing of buildings and more leasing, at least over the short term.
Stock control (mentioned below) may need to be questioned and
made the subject of training. The increase in debtors could require the
remedies mentioned above; training the credit control department,
involving the sales force in after-sales problem analysis, and so on.

When examining the accounts there are some simple, standard
tests that can be applied which may be small flags indicating a long
road to strategic change. We will consider the following:

APW Limited

Balance sheet as at 31st March 1989

	Cost	Accumulated depreciation	Net
	£	£	£
FIXED ASSETS			
Vehicles and fittings	2,000	1,000	1,000
PATENTS AND TRADEMARKS			1,000
			2,000
CURRENT ASSETS			
Stocks		1,000	
Debtors		500	
Bank and cash		500	
		2,000	

CURRENT LIABILITIES
Creditors	200	
Taxation	300	
Proposed dividend	500	
	1,000	

NET CURRENT ASSETS		1,000
		3,000

LONG TERM LIABILITIES
6 per cent debentures (secured)		(1,000)
		£2,000

represented by:
AUTHORISED AND ISSUED SHARE CAPITAL:
Ordinary shares of £1	1,000
CAPITAL RESERVE:	
Share premium	200
REVENUE RESERVE:	
Profit and loss balance	800
	£2,000

APW Limited

Profit and loss account for the year ended 31st March 1989

	£	£
SALES INCOME		12,000
Less: COST OF SALES		8,000
GROSS PROFIT		4,000
less: OVERHEADS		
Selling and distribution	1,500	
Administration and occupancy	700	
Directors' salaries	100	
Depreciation	440	
Debenture interest	60	
		2,800
NET PROFIT BEFORE TAX		1,200
TAXATION		300

	£	£
PROFIT AFTER TAX		900
PROPOSED DIVIDEND (of 50%)		500
RETAINED EARNINGS THIS YEAR		400
BALANCE FORWARD FROM LAST YEAR		400
CARRIED FORWARD PER BALANCE SHEET	£	800

Note: Market price of shares at the year end is £2 per share.

RATIO ANALYSIS

There are many ratios which can be examined in a company's accounts which indicate the health, or otherwise, of the company. None of these ratios is of any use by itself, but should be examined over a period of, say, five years and/or compared with similar companies in the same industry.

Gross profit percentage

$$\frac{\text{Gross profit}}{\text{Sales}} \times 100$$

Using the APW accounts: $\frac{£4,000}{£12,000} = 33\%$

An increase in gross profit percentage is a positive sign indicating that we are making more direct profit on the production and sale of our products. A fall in gross profit percentage would indicate that we were not able to demand the profit we used to be able to. There would still be questions to ask, however. If gross profit percentage was falling then we should ask the following questions.

1. Have sales revenues decreased because of falling selling prices? This would indicate that our products were not in the demand that they used to be and may be an indication that we are falling behind the times, and that our competitors are producing better products than us. Our company may be becoming old fashioned or 'stuck in its ways' and may need some very radical thinking to bring it up to date.

2. Has the sales revenue dropped because we have actually sold fewer items (as opposed to selling for less)? The indications could be the same as above. However, it could mean that we need to retrain the sales force; the market may be there but our people are behind the times in modern selling techniques. Our problem could be one of 'customer care'. The awareness of customers that they are 'in the driving seat' may not have reached the sales reps who think that people will have to buy what they are offered. Elsewhere in the book we refer to the recognition that the 'customer is king' – let's not forget to tell the sales force!

3. Has there been a change in the 'mix' of sales? This may mean that we make better gross profits on some of our product lines than others, but that it is the lower gross profit lines which are now in demand. The lines that have traditionally generated the most profit for us are now becoming unfashionable. We can very quickly find that the company becomes unviable as it can no longer depend on its traditional sales.

Net profit percentage

$$\frac{\text{Pretax net profit}}{\text{Sales}} \times 100$$

Using the APW accounts: $\frac{£1,200}{£12,000} = 10\%$

The net profit percentage is calculated after overhead costs have been deducted. Changes in the net profit percentage, ignoring changes caused by movements in the gross profit percentage above, indicate management control of the non-direct costs and fixed costs. An increase in gross profit percentage suggests either a good maintenance of overheads in the face of increasing activity or a reduction in overheads for the same level of activity. Equally, a decrease in net profit percentage indicates a deterioration or loss of control over the expenses.

A more detailed analysis of the individual overhead expenses should then be undertaken to determine areas of strength or weakness in management control. This can be done by examining the individual overheads against their corresponding figures of previous years and taking into account the known changes already undertaken within the company.

It may seem obvious, but introducing an effective, tight budgetary control in a company can be the most major change a company has seen in many years.

Many of these problems are, of course, simply a reflection of poor management and may not themselves indicate a need for change. However, our analysis of companies that have needed change programmes (whether they were farsighted enough to realise it or not) is that the earliest signs were in these sorts of accounts figures. In some cases they were simply a reflection of a tired management whose intangible effects were damaging the company, even if those effects were less easy to see.

Stock turnover

$$\frac{\text{Cost of sales}}{\text{Average stock}}$$

Using the APW accounts: $\dfrac{£8,000}{£1,000} = 8$ times

(This assumes that the stock is unchanged at the beginning and end of the year, at £1,000.)

This means that total stock is used and replaced, on average, eight times during the year. An increase in stock turnover rate suggests better efficiency of stock holding, i.e. less stock held. A decrease in stock turnover rate could be due to overstocking, or an accelerated degree of production or stocking to meet a known expansional growth.

Stock holding is a controversial subject and one that has been given much attention in recent years. The question of how much stock you should have is answered very simply: the minimum necessary. Money represented by the stock on the shelves is money tied up non-productively, and reduces the money available for day-to-day costs or interest earning investment. Furthermore, the stock held is costing money to hold. We have saved one company a great deal of money by changing its stock-holding policy to the point where it was able to sell off one of its warehouses, releasing considerable money for other uses.

Companies that are holding too much stock indicate a lack of awareness of current management thinking and a lack of sensible application of resources. As before, changing the stock-holding policy is not a 'change' issue as described in this book, but it is a common indicator that deeper, sometimes cultural, changes are needed.

Debt collection period

The formula is:

$$\frac{\text{Trade debtors}}{\text{Credit sales}} \times \underset{\text{(for months)}}{\frac{12}{1}} \quad \text{(or)} \quad \underset{\text{(for weeks)}}{\frac{52}{1}} \quad \text{(or)} \quad \underset{\text{(for days)}}{\frac{365}{1}}$$

In the APW example, assuming all sales are on credit then the calculation is:

$$\frac{£500}{£12,000} \times \underset{\text{(days)}}{\frac{365}{1}} = 15.21 \text{ days}$$

This means that debtors represent on average the last 15.21 days' sales.

A deteriorating debt collection period, i.e. an increase in figure, would indicate that our customers were not paying us as efficiently as they used to or that our own credit control department was not as efficient as it used to be.

It may indicate that we are having to sell our products to less reliable or less viable customers, because either the products themselves are less in demand or because our competition has broken into our traditional markets.

A change programme to ensure that we value our customers properly could well be indicated by this factor, alongside other evidence.

The working capital ratio

$$\frac{\text{Current assets}}{\text{Current liabilities}}$$

The example in APW Ltd is:

$$\frac{£2,000}{£1,000} = 2:1$$

The working capital ratio is an indicator of short-term liquidity and measures the ability of a business to meet its obligations as they fall due. The logic of the ratio is that current assets can be converted into cash (i.e. stock sold, debts collected) and the cash is used to meet current liabilities. For many companies a figure of 1.7:1 is traditionally regarded as desirable, though in certain businesses other factors may make a different figure normal. It is, as always, the changes over time that are significant.

Liquidity ratio (or acid test)

$$\frac{\text{Current assets less stock}}{\text{Current liabilities}}$$

In the APW Ltd example it is:

$$\frac{£1,000}{£1,000} = 1:1$$

The generally desirable figure is 0.7:1; any more would indicate a poor use of liquid assets and any less insufficient funds to pay debts as they fall due. The acid test is regarded as the most accurate predictor of bankruptcy: a deteriorating liquidity ratio indicating stretched resources.

There are certain indicators which reflect the way that the outside world (in particular speculative investors) sees the company. Other people's viewpoints are often very good indicators of a need for change.

Gearing

$$\frac{\text{Fixed interest loans}}{\text{Ordinary shares}}$$

In the APW example it is:

$$\frac{£1,000}{£1,000} = 1:1$$

The gearing ratio measures the degree to which the company is financed by fixed-interest borrowings and the degree to which it is financed by its owners. Fixed-interest loans require servicing, i.e. the interest and repayments have to be made regardless of profits and therefore strain the company's financial resources if profits are low. Dividends on the ordinary shares are only payable if there are profits from which to pay them and therefore do not strain the company's resources if profits are tight. (Types of preference shares can be either.)

An increase in gearing, i.e. an increased dependency on fixed-interest loans, makes a company more vulnerable in times of recession, for example. It possibly reflects the fact that individuals do not trust the company enough to invest their money in it on a speculative basis.

Short-term solutions to this problem have included, in recent times, persuading banks to convert debt to equity. In the longer term a change of strategy may be needed.

Earnings per share

$$\frac{\text{Profit after tax (in pence)}}{\text{Number of shares issued}}$$

In the APW example it is:

$$\frac{90,000 \text{ pence}}{1,000 \text{ pence}} = 90\text{p per share}$$

The earnings per share indicate the amount of money available for distribution to the shareholders. The higher the figure the better the dividends are likely to be. A decrease in earnings per share may indicate decrease in profits or a company that has been forced to issue more shares in order to find finance.

In recent times some companies have been forced to suspend their dividend payments to pay off debts, effectively reversing (under pressure from banks) the traditional equation of gearing. Other companies have opted for exchanging dividend for equity (issuing more shares instead of paying dividends). Such situations simply cannot exist for long or the share value of the company would collapse; a long-term strategy for change would be needed to address the fundamental problems.

The price/earnings (P/E) ratio

$$\frac{\text{Market price of share}}{\text{Earnings per share}}$$

In the APW example it is:

$$\frac{£2}{90\,p} = 2.2{:}1$$

This means that each share is valued at 2.2 × its earnings per share figure. An investor could pay £2 for a share and would expect to recover the entire investment in 2.2 years, and still have the investment paying dividends into the future. (It should be pointed out that these figures have all been exaggerated to demonstrate a point; no company would have such an earnings per share figure. The stock exchange would be swamped before its first quarter hour's trading should a company ever come on to the market in this state as there would be a surfeit of buyers and no sellers.) The price earnings ratio is the public's way of expressing confidence or lack of confidence in a company and its management. The market price of the share reflects the trust individuals would put in their investment.

Return on capital employed (ROCE)

There are many ways to define this ratio. For the sake of our example we will take:

$$\frac{\text{Net profit after tax}}{\text{Capital plus reserves}} \times 100$$

In the APW example that is:

$$\frac{£900}{£2,000} \times 100 = 45\%$$

A high ROCE probably shows a successful long-term growth and high profit margins. It is, of course, the time series analysis over a number of years which indicates whether or not the company is improving its return on capital employed or otherwise.

Specific profit and loss account items of expenditure

Advertising

If the company has reduced its advertising year on year it may indicate a lack of funds available or a lack of awareness about the need for marketing. Of course, if the company's sales are unaffected then it may well mean that the previous marketing was ineffective or that the company has little need at the present time to market (this is very rarely the case).

Advertising is often one of the first expenses in a company to be cut back in times of struggling cash flows. This may represent a short-term view as market share can be lost.

By the same token an increase in advertising may indicate that the company is struggling to sell its products and may be losing its market share for one reason or another.

Advertising, therefore, is one of the first indications of management decisions and may suggest an area of investigation. Movements in advertising budgets would not be of value without knowing some background information about the reason.

Training

Because training is not reflected on the bottom line, i.e. since at least in theory the company can produce and sell the same products or services with or without training, training is also one of the early items to be cut back in times of recession. Cutting back on training may indicate a short-term view which is usually detrimental over a medium or long term.

Capital expenditure

Is the company keeping up with current technology or falling behind competitors who, using current technology, may be able to produce the products at a cheaper unit cost and therefore undercut the company in the market? The company's capital expenditure programme often reflects the company's attitude towards its long-term goals.

IF MONEY IS NOT THE MEASURE

There are areas inside a company that have traditionally served as indicators of a need for change. Like the financial indicators these have been identified, sadly, from those collapsed companies whose bones we – and others – have picked apart. The need for companies to be proactive to change rather than reactive means that these areas should also be regularly considered.

Customers

You should review the customer base of the company and examine whether or not it has increased its spread of customers. The more customers a company has the less dependent it is on a collapse in another company and the less vulnerable it is to losing customers to the competition. Companies which 'rest on their laurels' may find themselves vulnerable to their own customer companies if they also rest on their laurels. Old-fashioned companies going out of business take old-fashioned clients with them. New companies will be entering the market place and your company should be seeking them out as potential customers.

Suppliers

In almost exactly the same way as we look at customers, we should be looking for new sources of supply at all times. There will be companies coming into the market who will be able to supply us more cost-effectively than our traditional suppliers. We should be looking for technological and other progress in our suppliers, as well as in ourselves.

Product launches

When did the company last launch a new product? If it has been some time since that happened, it may be that we are falling behind the times. Even companies that successfully sold the same product for decades have often found that new technologies suddenly make those products out of date. At the present time there is a move towards cheap, computerised packages for accounts preparation for small businesses. They can be used on relatively inexpensive personal computers. As they become more prevalent, so the traditional, bookkeeping registers that have sold since the beginning of the century will become in very limited demand.

Staff turnover

There is, in recent years, a trend towards more mobility of employment. The concept of wanting a 'job for life' even if it was available is rarer now than, say, fifty years ago. Some American management studies recommend a total career change every ten years. Certainly, employers are often interested in the person who has had a variety of job experience rather than the 'loyal' employee who was with his or her last firm for twenty years.

However, if the company is suffering a high turnover of staff, or a higher turnover than former years, it may indicate that there is something in need of change. Perhaps the company is not recognised as being state of the art any longer and the 'best' people are looking elsewhere for employment. That would be a typical indicator in the advertising industry, for example. It may just be that caring for employees is getting out of date; the company is not keeping up with current trends of looking after its staff. If staff turnover is increasing due to the dissatisfaction of the employees, then that is reason enough for a change programme of sorts. However, it may also indicate a lack of awareness in other areas and a look at the treatment of suppliers and customers, and soon becomes a necessary next step.

Age of the management team

It is useful to consider the average age of the management team and whether it is getting too high. This is not at all to say that people are necessarily of no use when they get older; companies are just beginning to realise that experience is a prize to be valued. The 'yuppies' of the 1980s proved to be glittering fireworks, but fireworks that burnt out quickly.

However, new ideas need new minds. The management team, inasmuch as it should not necessarily be getting younger, should also not let itself get older. New blood should be brought on board.

In one company where we consulted we dealt with a common problem; getting the first generation out so that the next generation (their sons for the most part) could take over. Wisely, the first generation were retained as consultants and proved to be useful as such. But the management team's average age ended up almost the same as it had been when the company had started some forty years ago; it had been getting steadily older and this rectified that balance.

Benchmarking

Another tool available to management to identify the need for change, which is being increasingly used by manufacturing industry, is benchmarking. Here, the efficiency of the organisation is measured by calculating the numbers of work-force, staff and management, and comparing those numbers with those in similar organisations.

One company might ask, for example, why does it take 450 staff, 25 middle managers and 10 senior managers to produce product X, when another company is achieving the same result with 350 staff, 17 middle managers and 5 senior managers? Benchmarking compares one organisation with, say, half a dozen others. Using graphics such as bar charts, easily understood comparisons can be communicated to all levels of the organisation.

The challenge of benchmarking is therefore not just to consider the numbers of people employed, but the grades and hierarchical positions in which they are employed to achieve a given result.

The problem of benchmarking is to be sure that you are comparing like with like; all companies have certain unique factors. Benchmarking can be used to compare companies, departments, sites and so on.

Benchmarking is often referred to as 'best in class' and although somewhat primitive it does offer a yardstick by which the organisation can construct its longer term strategies.

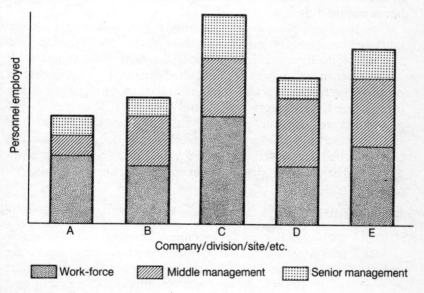

Figure 14.1
Typical benchmarking bar-chart

The assumption is that all five (A,B,C,D,E) units are producing the same output.

In this example A might be regarded as 'best of class' and the

benchmark target for others to aim at to make the most effective use
of their personnel.

THE EFFECT OF RECESSION

As the 1980/1990s recession has demonstrated, many of the more
elaborate change programmes (customer care, total quality and so
on) can be forced to take a back seat in favour of these very
simplistic changes when survival is at stake. In Chapter 8 we
pointed out that when basic, low-level needs such as housing and
food are threatened people revert to primitive responses; companies are no different.

15 | *DIAGRAMMATIC TOOLS OF PROJECT MANAGEMENT*

Change programmes are projects pretty much like any others in that they need to be planned, divided into manageable 'chunks' and executed systematically. The usual, and the special, considerations that apply to change programmes are included in the various chapters of the book.

However, there are two useful tools for project management that it will be useful to record here; diagrammatic ways of setting out the whole project in order that individual areas can be seen in perspective. These are particularly useful for people who have not been involved in change, or other, projects before. As we have pointed out in Parts I and II, change agents are usually people with certain qualities selected for the task, but who may never before have been exposed to such a level of management information. They may feel overwhelmed by the data.

The first chart – of critical path analysis – is a diagrammatic way of showing why certain tasks must be performed within certain times if the whole programme is not to be delayed. It may be easiest for the change agents to use such diagrams when explaining this problem to others.

The second chart – the Gantt chart – is a useful way of displaying the whole picture for those involved, and for showing the areas where resources will be most stretched.

CRITICAL PATH ANALYSIS (CPA)

The essence of CPA is to determine which activities cannot be started until others have been completed, and which activities can be dealt with while others are progressing. By planning the times needed to deal with each of these tasks a critical path can be calculated. The critical path is the longest time needed to get through the network of interrelated jobs. By way of simple example, if there are two tasks to be done at the same time for completion of a project, one taking one day and another two days, then the project cannot be completed in under two days. Furthermore, the task that takes one day can overrun by as much as 100 per cent (to two days) without affecting the overall project time, whereas the other task must not overrun at all, or the whole project will be delayed. Once identified, and displayed on a Gantt chart, appropriate resources can be allocated to the critical path to ensure that the overall project remains in time budget.

Critical path analysis is best explained by way of example.

Information: Activity:	Duration: (days)
A: document current handling procedures in the dept	3
B: prepare flowchart of systems	4
C: discuss systems with outside consultants	5
D: discuss with staff their problems of paper handling	6
E: discuss flowchart with senior management	2
F: discuss flowchart with systems designers	1
G: discuss recommendations with senior management	7
H: list adjustments needed for new system	4
I: briefing sessions with staff on new systems	3
J: devise improved paper-handling procedures	5
K: devise remedies to staff problems	6
L: design flowcharts of new system	2

Activity(s):	Depends on the completion of activity(s):
B, C and D	A
E and F	B
G	E
H	F
I	G and H
J	G, H, C and D
K	D
L	I, J and K

The critical path chart would look like this:

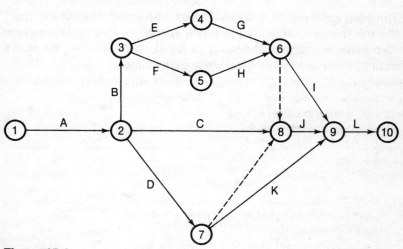

Figure 15.1
Critical path chart

The various 'routes' through the chart are as follows:

A B E G I L	21 days
A B E G Dummy J L	23 days
A B F H I L	17 days
A B F H Dummy J L	19 days
A C J L	15 days
A D Dummy I L	16 days
A D K L	17 days

Clearly, the critical path, the longest route, is the one taking twenty-three days. Tasks on this route must be completed in time if the project is not to be delayed; tasks not on the critical path can be allowed to falter if necessary. Maximum resources would be allocated to the tasks on the critical path in order to keep the project on target.

GANTT CHARTS

The same tasks can be displayed on a Gantt chart. The advantage of these is that they are easy to follow, and allow for resources available to be set against the tasks in hand. The tasks in our above example would look like this on a Gantt chart:

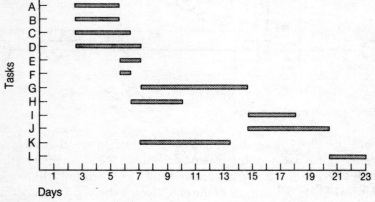

Figure 15.2
Gantt chart

Against the chart above we can then allocate available resources. For the sake of simplicity let us assume that five people will be available throughout the project. There will be times when they will not all be needed, and there will be times when five is not enough. In the circumstances where there are not enough, more people could be brought in to supplement the team if the tasks were on the critical path. The chart, with resource allocations, would look like this:

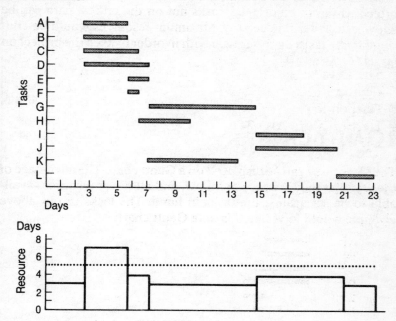

Figure 15.3
With resource allocations

What the chart now shows is that although there is a constant availability of five people (shown by the line ················), they will not always be needed and can sometimes be released for other work. This is the case along most of the chart where the people needed are fewer than five. However, there is a time lasting four days when seven people are needed. Since some of the tasks are on the critical path, it may be necessary to devote additional resources to those days in order to keep the project on target.

The chart is also a simple and effective way of displaying the tasks as a part of the whole.

John Spencer and Adrian Pruss jointly run APW Training.

APW Training can be contacted at:

The Leys
Leyton Road
Harpenden
Hertfordshire AL5 2TL

Telephone: (0582) 468592
Fax   : (0582) 461979

INDEX

Piatkus Business Books

Piatkus Business Books have been created for people like you, busy executives and managers who need expert knowledge readily available in a clear and easy-to-follow format. All the books are written by specialists in their field. They will help you improve your skills quickly and effortlessly in the workplace and on a personal level. Titles include:

General Management Skills

Be Your Own PR Expert: The Complete Guide to Publicity and Public Relations   Bill Penn

Brain Power: The 12-Week Mental Training Programme   Marilyn vos Savant and Leonore Fleischer

The Complete Time Management System   Christian H. Godefroy and John Clark

Confident Decision Making   J. Edward Russo and Paul J. H. Schoemaker

Dealing with Difficult People   Roberta Cava

The Energy Factor: How to Motivate Your Workforce   Art McNeil

Firing On All Cylinders: Tried and Tested Techniques to Improve the Performance of Your Organisation   Jim Clemmer with Barry Sheehy

How to Develop and Profit from Your Creative Powers   Michael LeBoeuf

The Influential Manager: How to use Company Politics Constructively   Lee Bryce

Leadership Skills for Every Manager   Jim Clemmer and Art McNeil

Lure the Tiger Out of the Mountains: How to Apply the 36 Stratagems of Ancient China to the Modern World   Gao Yuan

Managing Your Team   John Spencer and Adrian Pruss

Problem Employees   Peter Wylie and Mardy Grothe

Psychological Testing for Managers   Dr Stephanie Jones

Sales and Customer Services

The Art of the Hard Sell   Robert L. Shook

How to Close Every Sale   Joe Girard

How to Succeed in Network Marketing   Leonard Hawkins

How to Win Customers and Keep Them for Life   Michael LeBoeuf

Sales Power: The Silva Mind Method for Sales Professionals   José Silva and Ed Bernd Jr

Selling by Direct Mail   John W. Graham and Susan K. Jones

Telephone Selling Techniques that Really Work   Bill Good

Presentation and Communication

Better Business Writing Maryann V. Piotrowski

The Complete Book of Business Etiquette Lynne Brennan and David Block

Confident Conversation: How to Talk in any Business or Social Situation Dr Lillian Glass

Powerspeak: The Complete Guide to Public Speaking and Presentation Dorothy Leeds

The Power Talk System: How to Communicate Effectively Christian H. Godefroy and Stephanie Barrat

Personal Power: How to Achieve Influence and Success in Your Professional Life Philippa Davies

Say What You Mean and Get What You Want George R. Walther

Your Total Image: How to Communicate Success Philippa Davies

Careers

The Influential Woman: How to Achieve Success Without Losing Your Femininity Lee Bryce

Marketing Yourself: How to Sell Yourself and Get the Jobs You've Always Wanted Dorothy Leeds

Networking and Mentoring: A Woman's Guide Dr Lily Segerman-Peck

Which Way Now? How to Plan and Develop a Successful Career Bridget Wright

The Perfect CV: How to Get the Job You Really Want Tom Jackson

Ten Steps to the Top Marie Jennings

Small Business

The Best Person for the Job: Where to Find Them and How to Keep Them Malcolm Bird

How to Collect the Money You Are Owed Malcolm Bird

Making Profits: A Six-Month Plan for the Small Business Malcolm Bird

Organize Yourself Ronni Eisenberg and Kate Kelly

For a free brochure with further information on our complete range of business titles, please write to:

Piatkus Books
Freepost 7 (WD 4505)
London W1E 4EZ

PIATKUS

MANAGING YOUR TEAM

by John Spencer and Adrian Pruss

MANAGING YOUR TEAM is packed with information and advice for everyone who is responsible for building a team or improving its performance.

Find out how to:
- Negotiate a team contract
- Select the right people
- Understand the stages of team development
- Focus your team towards a common goal
- Motivate your team for maximum results

John Spencer and Adrian Pruss are principal trainers of APW Training. John Spencer is a qualified accountant, business trainer, management consultant and author. Adrian Pruss has worked as a trainer and consultant to companies all over the world.

THE COMPLETE TIME MANAGEMENT SYSTEM

by Christian H. Godefroy and John Clark

The Complete Time Management System will change the way you work and think. It will increase your enjoyment of life and your chances of success. It will show you:

- How to do in 2 hours what you usually need 4 hours to do
- How to revive your concentration
- How to read 240 pages an hour
- How to make an important decision faster
- How to delegate
- How to organise your office
- How to shorten meetings
- And much, much more

Learn the secrets of time management and you will profit from them all your life.

Christian Godefroy is a training specialist, founder of a publishing company in France and best-selling author.

THE INFLUENTIAL MANAGER

by Lee Bryce

THE INFLUENTIAL MANAGER is for all managers and aspiring managers who want to rise up the career ladder. Based on a sound understanding of human psychology and organisational politics, it shows you how to:

- Become a powerful person at work, without squashing or alienating your colleagues
- Use your power and influence to empower other people and become a first-class manager
- Play office politics constructively, and with integrity

Lee Bryce is a director of Denham Nash, her own human resources management consultancy which runs training courses for several top companies and organisations.

LEADERSHIP SKILLS FOR EVERY MANAGER

by Jim Clemmer and Art McNeil

Leadership Skills for Every Manager offers the key to organisational effectiveness. It shows you how to:

- Develop leadership skills throughout your company
- Examine the four leadership elements – vision, values, environment and behaviour – that exist in every organisation
- Build powerful and effective teams
- Align organisational culture
- Train people towards higher personal performance
- Transform good intentions into concrete results

Executives, managers and supervisors will find *Leadership Skills for Every Manager* an invaluable catalyst for action.

Jim Clemmer and Art McNeil are founders and operating executives of The Achieve Group, which specialises in leadership development and organisational effectiveness.

DEALING WITH DIFFICULT PEOPLE

by Roberta Cava

Dealing with Difficult People contains proven strategies for handling stressful situations and defusing tensions. Discover how to:

- Deal with specific problems and personality conflicts
- Increase your people skills and work better with others
- Identify the main cause of customer frustration and anger – and how to alleviate it
- Work better with your boss, colleagues and subordinates
- Reduce your own stress and anxiety and increase your confidence

Roberta Cava runs her own management consulting firm which specialises in training and development seminars on interpersonal skills, assertiveness, time and stress management and personal and business development.

PROBLEM EMPLOYEES

by Peter Wylie and Mardy Grothe

PROBLEM EMPLOYEES offers a better way to manage one of business's most tricky issues – dealing with difficult staff. Packed with examples, scenarios and step-by-step procedures, it shows you how to deal with an employee who:

- alienates co-workers and customers
- is unwilling to work a minute more than required
- lacks motivation
- shows signs of drug or alcohol abuse
- challenges your authority

Dr Peter Wylie and Dr Mardy Grothe are partners in Performance Improvement Associates, which runs successful courses and workshops for managers and supervisors.